# CROWOOD SPORTS GUIDES
# BOWLS
## SKILLS • TECHNIQUES • TACTICS

John Bell

THE CROWOOD PRESS

First published in 2007 by
The Crowood Press Ltd
Ramsbury, Marlborough
Wiltshire SN8 2HR

www.crowood.com

British Library Cataloguing-in-Publication Data
A catalogue record for this book is available from the British Library.

ISBN 978 1 86126 968 3

## Disclaimer

Please note that the author and the publisher of this book are not responsible in any manner whatsoever for any damage, or injury of any kind, that may result from practising, or applying, the techniques and methods and/or following the instructions described in this publication. Since the warm-up exercises and other physical activities described in this book may be too strenuous in nature for some readers to engage in safely, it is essential that a doctor be consulted prior to undertaking such exercises and activities.

Throughout this book 'he', 'him' and 'his' are used as neutral pronouns and as such refer to males and females.

## Captions for Part opening pictures:

Part 1, p.7 David Bryant CBE is the world's most accomplished bowler, having been three times Outdoor and Indoor World Singles Champion and four times Commonwealth Games Singles Champion. He is an everlasting icon of the game. (Courtesy of *Bowls International*)

Part 2, p.33 Tony Allcock MBE is one of the finest bowlers to grace the game. In his career he has won back-to-back World Outdoor Singles titles and been World Indoor Singles Champion three times. (Courtesy of *Bowls International*)

Part 3, p.81 Alex Marshall MBE is a true world superstar, with a record four World Indoor Singles titles to his credit, as well as being a back-to-back Commonwealth Games Pairs Champion and a World Outdoor Pairs and Fours Champion and Indoor Pairs winner. (Courtesy of *Bowls International*)

Part 4, p.115 Ellen Falkner, another talented rising star. As well as twice winner of the Ladies' World Indoor Singles Championship, she was a Gold Medallist in the England fours team at the 2002 Commonwealth Games and the Ladies World Championships in 2004. (Courtesy of *Bowls International*)

Photograph previous page: Andy Thomson: a World Indoor and Outdoor Champion, and a perfect role model for excellent technique.

Line drawings by Keith Field.

Typeset and designed by
D & N Publishing, Lambourn Woodlands, Hungerford, Berkshire.

Printed and bound in Singapore by Craft Print International.

# CROWOOD SPORTS GUIDES

# BOWLS

ACTICS

# CONTENTS

# FOREWORD

Bowls is a fairly simple game with all participants having one primary aim: to get the bowl near to the jack. Whatever the degree of science applied, the objectives remain the same. In this guide, John Bell fully acknowledges this and reminds the reader that, whether one is a World Class performer or a raw beginner, the fundamental rules always apply. The greater the skill acquired, the easier the basic principles may be forgotten.

The author, in utilizing his vast experience of playing and managing bowls at the highest level, will assist every bowls coach and student of this sport to study carefully the recommendations, which adequately apply to all bowlers. With improved skill there must, automatically, come renewed enthusiasm from every bowler to play to their best ability and to ultimately achieve their goal.

Happy reading!

Tony Allcock MBE

# ACKNOWLEDGEMENTS

The Author and publishers would like to thank the following for their help and cooperation in the production of this book: Lynne Rowley, for her untiring typing services; Stuart Airey, for his classic demonstration skills; Paul Walker, for capturing them so well on camera; Cumbria Indoor Bowls Club, for kindly accommodating our photo sessions; Melvyn Beck and *Bowls International* magazine, for supplying the excellent archive photos and various invaluable pieces of information; Rex Hazeldine, for his warm-up routines; and the English Bowling Association, World Bowls Ltd and the English Bowls Coaching Scheme for their assistance.

# DEDICATION

To my wife Jeanette, and our Emma and John – a massive thank you. From quality control to inspiring suggestions, they have contributed and supported me during the production of this book, as they have done throughout my bowling career. I have immense pleasure in dedicating this book to them, two of whom, I am delighted to report, are now accomplished bowlers in their own right.

*The author, John Bell.*

# PART I
# INTRODUCTION
# TO BOWLS

# CHAPTER 1

# DEVELOPMENT OF THE GAME

## Proud History

It is contended by certain chronicles that bowling is the oldest outdoor sport in the world – some form of bowling, that is, because the term has embraced games that are more allied to skittles than lawn bowls. Nevertheless, it is known that as early as 5200BC the Chinese rolled stones to a hole in the ground with the object of getting as near to the lip as possible. There is also a picture of bowls being played in Egypt around 300BC, from where the sport spread to Greece and Rome. It made its way to Northern Europe around the tenth century and onward into Britain. Could it be that our term 'bowls' is derived from the Latin word *bulla,* used for ball games in general? The Aztecs too indulged in a similar game.

The date of its introduction remains unknown, but a bowling green is mentioned in the records of Chichester Castle soon after 1066. Christchurch claims its bowling origins date back to 1100 and Bedford Priory to 1220, whilst Southampton Bowling Club was founded in 1299. We can be certain that a type of bowls as we know it, depicted in the earliest known drawing of bowls in the Royal Library at Windsor, was played in England during the thirteenth century.

Edward I (1272–1307) was the first English monarch to play bowls. Royalty and landed gentry had greens built on their own estates, but at large the game was played on areas of turf associated with taverns and inns. It became very popular, in fact too popular, and attracted severe criticism for creating serious social problems. One report describes the game as attracting 'dissolute persons, betting, drunkenness, quarrelling and even duelling'. It was even seen to be undermining the country's security as players were spending too much time bowling and not enough improving their archery skills, which were required for national defence. The monarchy was therefore called upon to suppress the game: Edward III, and later Richard II in 1388, passed laws forbidding bowls and other sports. Anyone caught in the act was liable to two years in prison and a fine of £10.

Henry VIII gave the sport a little respite in 1541 by signing a statute, which stayed on the books until 1845, allowing 'artificers, labourers, apprentices and servants to play bowls at Christmas – but only in their master's house and presence'. The wealthier gentry could play within their own gardens and orchards but only under licence; if they played outside their own premises they were liable to a fine of six shillings and eight pence.

Henry himself enjoyed a game of bowls and had his own green at Hampton Court, where records show that large gambling bets were placed. This practice became so popular that a clause was added to the statute of 1541 to stop greens being established for gain. By that time he would probably have been playing with biased bowls, following an incident at Goole on 31 March 1522 that was to change the face of bowls and literally shape it to the game we know today. The Duke of Suffolk delivered his bowl with such force that it shattered into tiny pieces. Determined to continue, he went inside and espied a large wooden ornamental knob at the bottom of his banisters. He took a saw, removed it and returned to his game.

The new 'bowl', needless to say, took a curved line reflecting its sawn shape. The day of the biased bowl had dawned.

The more liberal attitude of Henry VIII and his son Edward VI was quickly replaced by a less tolerant Queen Mary in 1553. Two years after her succession she withdrew all bowling licences, deeming the game an excuse for 'unlawful assemblies, conventions, seditions and conspiracies'. Indeed the game was considered to be of questionable repute for the rest of the sixteenth century, although things must have relaxed somewhat by 1588 when Drake played his much celebrated, and published, game on Plymouth Hoe.

The seventeenth century saw the game receive much greater royal patronage. Charles I enjoyed the sport and gambled heavily on his games. He even had a green laid for him while he was a prisoner in Carisbrooke Castle. His son Charles II was an even bigger bowling devotee, and the game's first royal administrator. Together with his brother James, Duke of York, and the Duke of Birmingham he drew up a new set of rules in 1670 for the regulation and standardization of the game. Before his time the rules of play varied from green to green. Interestingly, one of these new laws was 'always keep your temper'.

Early settlers to the new colonies also took their bowls with them. Bowling was a popular pastime in New York in the eighteenth century, where there is still a park in Manhattan called Bowling Green and a stained-glass window in a nearby building vividly depicts the art of bowls. Boston, too, was a popular venue for bowls, though the 'Boston Tea Party' and the subsequent war of independence ensured that the British game lost favour overnight. The game was also taken to Australia with the early fleets and the first reported bowls match was at Sandy Bay, Hobart, in 1845.

Nearer to home the game had been thriving in Scotland since early in the seventeenth century. It was the Scots who continued where Charles II had left off and produced the most comprehensive set of rules to date, courtesy of a Glasgow solicitor called William Mitchell. These were to come into general use and were adopted in many countries. By 1888 there were 364 clubs in Scotland and in 1892 the Scottish Bowling Association was formed.

Not to be left behind, this enthusiasm seems to have overflowed into England. Coupled with the interest that was now being expressed by the famous all-rounder Dr W. G. Grace, the climate was almost right for the inauguration of a national administrative body. In 1899 games were arranged with Australian bowlers who were accompanying an Aussie cricket team then touring England. A man called S. Yelland set to work on the feasibility of arranging formal games against Australia. This led to the formation of the Imperial Bowling Association specifically to undertake the task. The London County Bowling Club and Association played against Scotland in 1901, allowing W. G. Grace to learn more about the Scottish Association. The fixture was deemed a great success and Grace subsequently promoted the idea that international matches should be instituted for the home countries. The arrangements for them to be held in London on 13–15 July 1903 were concluded by the previous April. The hosting of this prestigious event was in no small part responsible for focusing attention on the formation of the English Bowling Association on 8 June 1903.

This was duly followed by national associations across the globe. Bowls today is truly an international sport with 52 member national authorities in 45 member nations. It is a core sport in the Commonwealth Games and holds its own outdoor World Championship event every four years.

## Bowls Today

Welcome to our great game of bowls. It can be many things to very many people. It is enjoyed by young and old, male and female, and reaches out to members of the local community from all walks of life. It can be a competitive sport, a therapeutic recreation or a relaxing social pastime. Starting with the humble roll ups at my home club in Wigton, Cumbria, at the age of twelve, bowls has subsequently taken me round the world several times. En route I have had the pleasure and privilege of playing in and winning World, European and British championships.

Many thousands of bowlers, however, are just as happy to play social bowls at their own and neighbouring clubs. Our game is one that can satisfy the needs and aspirations of all that participate in it. The level at which the individual chooses to play is entirely his or her choice. It can be as competitive or as recreational as you want it to be.

Whatever level that may be, you can rest assured that the wonderful social environment and the high standard of behaviour and sportsmanship surrounding our game will enhance your valued leisure time.

### Flat Green Bowls – Part of a Family

This book concentrates exclusively on the 'flat green' game of bowls as played throughout the world and administered by World Bowls Ltd and the World Indoor Bowls Council. There are, however, other derivations of the game that function successfully alongside that discipline.

Crown Green bowls, Federation bowls, Short Mat and Carpet bowls all have their own distinctive individual variations of play and governing bodies. Contact details and a brief explanation of their nature are set out in the Appendix.

*Popular championship events are now worldwide. This is the Australian Open.*
*(© John Bell)*

CHAPTER 2

# GETTING STARTED

## Joining a Club

Whatever experience or motivation has
sparked your interest in the noble art of
bowls you are well advised to pursue that
interest through joining a bowling club.
There are more than 3,700 outdoor clubs
and over 425 indoor bowls clubs
throughout Great Britain. The vast majority
have qualified coaches to assist you make
a successful transition from novice to
competent performer.

Clubs welcome new members. Many
have facilities that provide for a very
attractive social environment to run

alongside the playing side. Entry fees and
annual subscriptions are usually modest.
Few other sports can offer so much playing
time and social activity for so little outlay.

Should you wish to play bowls
throughout the year you will probably
need to join both an indoor club and an
outdoor club. Some clubs have both
indoor and outdoor playing facilities, but
they are few in number, so it is more likely
that you will join two clubs. Outdoor play
ceases in September when remedial work
is undertaken on the greens to enable
them to recover from the intensive play of
the summer season. They will reopen

during the following April. Indoor play is
normally undertaken during the time
(September–April) when the outdoor
greens are closed.

The club(s) you join will almost
certainly come under the jurisdiction of a
County Association, which in turn comes
under the rules and auspices of its
national association. Individual clubs
organize their own domestic competitions
and social bowls programmes, including
matches against other clubs. These are for
the exclusive benefit of its members. The
formats involved with club competitions
need not necessarily mirror those

*A bowls club – the focal point for your enjoyment of both bowls action and the associated social activity.*

*The spacious and picturesque Llandrindod Wells Outdoor Bowls Club.*
*(Courtesy of Bowls International)*

organized at national and county level. For the more competitive minded, each member of the club is affiliated to the national body and as such can enter the annual national competitions. These are normally played at county/area level as the first stage, with the winner/qualifiers going on to represent the county/area in the annual national championships.

## Choosing a Club

The location of clubs can usually be found through information centres or by contacting the national governing bodies, who will be able to provide you with a contact number for County Associations, or even individual club contacts in your area. There are several factors you may wish to consider when choosing a club. These should include:

- How much time do you have available?
- Do you wish to play socially or competitively?
- How many teams does the club have?
- What does the club's social bowls programme consist of?

*Club action at the Scarborough Indoor Bowls Club.*
*(Courtesy of Bowls International)*

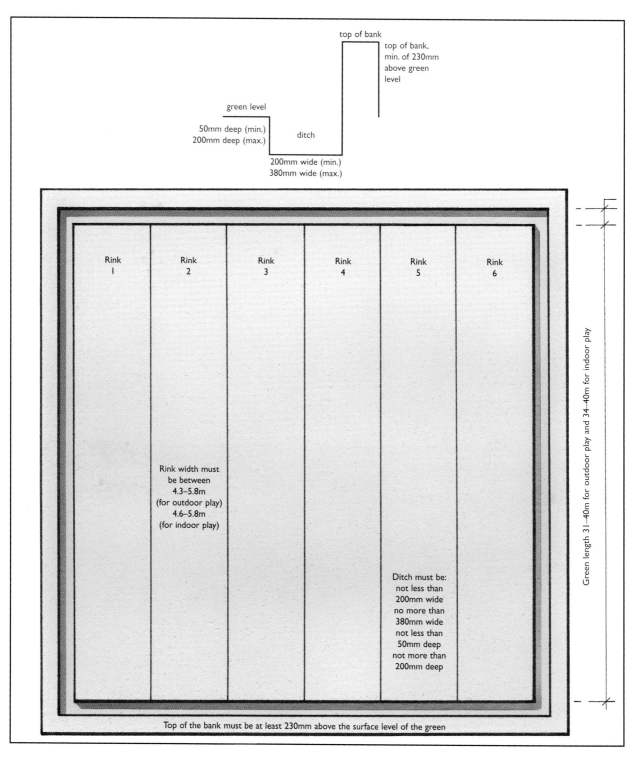

top of bank

top of bank,
min. of 230mm
above green
level

green level

50mm deep (min.)
200mm deep (max.)

ditch

200mm wide (min.)
380mm wide (max.)

Rink
1

Rink
2

Rink
3

Rink
4

Rink
5

Rink
6

Rink width must
be between
4.3–5.8m
(for outdoor play)
4.6–5.8m
(for indoor play)

Ditch must be:
not less than
200mm wide
no more than
380mm wide
not less than
50mm deep
not more than
200mm deep

Green length 31–40m for outdoor play and 34–40m for indoor play

Top of the bank must be at least 230mm above the surface level of the green

Fig 1   The Green: divided into individual playing areas called rinks.

- Is the playing surface of the green in good condition?
- What facilities does the club have and what are its opening hours?
- Is the club (and its clubhouse) open all year round?
- Is coaching available?
- How many members does the club have?
- What is the average age of the members?
- Is the club affiliated to the national governing body?
- What is the cost of membership and match fees?
- What is the general standard of play and how does it compare to yours?
- How long will it take you to get from home/work to the club? (Evening games often commence at 6.30pm, which makes accessibility an important factor).

## The Laws of the Sport

Players should familiarize themselves with the complete 'Laws of the Sport of Bowls' as a matter of course. These are published by the world governing bodies – World Bowls Ltd and World Indoor Bowls Council – in association with the individual national governing bodies. They are shown in full on the former's websites and printed copies can also be purchased for a nominal sum from the latter. Contact details are all shown in Appendix 1.

This section contains a simplified description of what the game involves, and how it is played. The various terms and expressions commonly used in the game, and frequently quoted below, are explained in the Glossary, to which you should refer as you read this introductory section. It will help you to get a good initial understanding of the rudiments of the game of bowls.

### The Basic Principles

Bowls games can be played between two people (2 × singles), four people (2 × pairs), six people (2 × triples) and eight people (2 × fours). Team games can also be played. These normally involve six fours

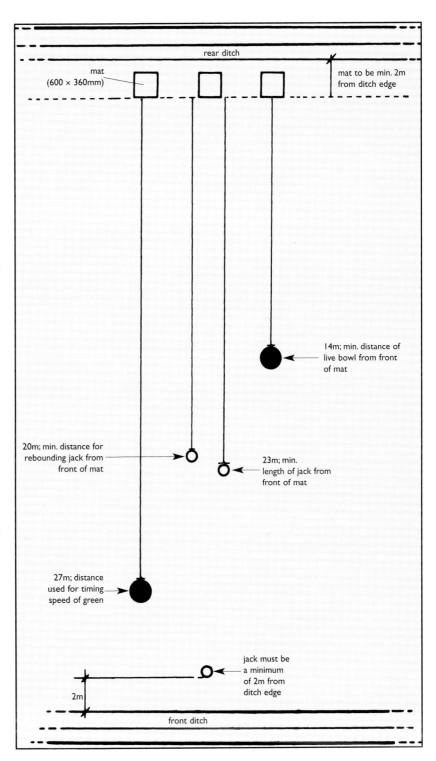

Fig 2 Minimum lengths and distances.

per side, but other variations can also occur. These may involve a smaller number of fours, or triples instead, a combination of individual disciplines, or a smaller number of disciplines.

## The Green

The game of bowls is played on a green, which can be indoors or outdoors. The length of the green in the direction of play should be between 34m (32m indoors) and 40m. The green must be surrounded by a ditch with a bank against its outer edge.

The green is divided into parallel sections to provide individual playing areas called 'rinks'. Sometimes strings are used to demarcate the boundaries of the rinks. Individual games are played within the confines of each of these rinks (see Fig 1).

Each player will play with up to four bowls, depending on what type of game is being played: singles (4 bowls); pairs (4 bowls each); triples (3 bowls each) and fours (2 bowls each).

## Playing your Backhand and Forehand

You will deliver your bowls standing on a mat, which must be at least 2m from the edge of the ditch. You will deliver your bowls down either side of the rink. Assuming you are right-handed, if you deliver them down the left-hand side of the rink (as you look at the jack) this is known as playing the 'backhand'. The other side of the rink – the right-hand side – is the forehand. If you are left-handed the opposite applies (the left-hand side of the rink is your forehand, and the right-hand side your backhand).

These are the two 'hands' you will have the choice of playing in both directions in all games.

## The Jack

You will hope your bowls finish as near as possible to a white spherical ball (63/64mm in diameter). This is commonly

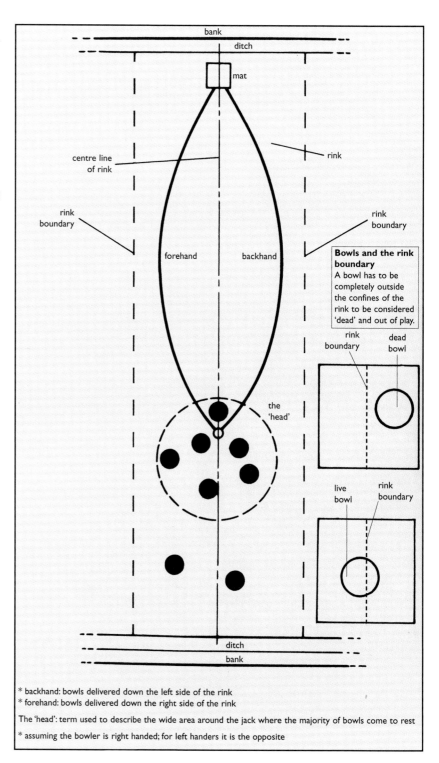

Fig 3 *Illustration of common bowling terms.*

Within the figure:
bank
ditch
mat
centre line of rink
rink
rink boundary
rink boundary
forehand
backhand
**Bowls and the rink boundary**
A bowl has to be completely outside the confines of the rink to be considered 'dead' and out of play.
rink boundary
dead bowl
the 'head'
live bowl
rink boundary
ditch
bank

* backhand: bowls delivered down the left side of the rink
* forehand: bowls delivered down the right side of the rink

The 'head': term used to describe the wide area around the jack where the majority of bowls come to rest

* assuming the bowler is right handed; for left handers it is the opposite

known as the 'jack', 'white' or 'kitty'. It must always be at least 23m away from the mat, at least 2m from the facing ditch edge, and positioned on the centre line of the rink.

The 'jack' always starts on the centreline of the rink at the commencement of each end. It may, of course, be subsequently knocked or trailed away from the centre line. This is all part and parcel of the game as long as it stays within the confines of the rink (see Figs 2 and 3).

## The Head

The object of the game is simple – to get more of your bowls close to the 'jack' than your opponent over a specified period. The area around the 'jack', where the majority of bowls come to rest, is called the 'head'. It is a commonly used, yet arbitrary, term describing an area with no finite boundaries. Its extent is open to individual interpretation.

## Live and Dead Bowls and Jacks

A delivered bowl must travel at least 14m from the front of the mat for it to be considered a live bowl. The jack and bowls must also always remain within the confines of the 'rink' if they are to play any part in the game. If the jack is knocked outside the rink boundaries, or over the bank, it is considered 'dead' and the end must be replayed. (Certain competition rules allow the jack to be re-spotted on the rink instead of replaying the end, but such practice is not widespread. If it is re-spotted, it is normally placed 1m in from the rink boundary and 2m from the ditch.) If the jack is knocked into the ditch within the confines of the rink, it is still considered to be alive and play can continue. Likewise, a bowl that touches the jack and finishes in the ditch is also deemed to be 'live' and can remain in the ditch, after being 'chalked' to indicate that it is still live. Bowls entering the ditch without touching the jack are 'dead' and must be removed onto the bank. Bowls finishing outside the confines of the rink, whether they have touched the jack or not, are also 'dead'. Such a bowl must be entirely outside the rink boundary. If any part of it, however small, is within or above the rink boundary it is still considered to be in play. This also applies to the jack. Optical devices are sometimes used to line up with the rink boundary markers in order to adjudge whether bowls and jacks are still in play. Alternatively a string can be laid along the line of the rink boundary to determine the exact position of a bowl or jack there.

## Rebounding Bowls and Jacks

If the jack is driven against the bank and comes back onto the rink it remains in play as long as it is at least 20m from the front of the mat (and still within the confines of the rink). Similarly, if a bowl hits the jack and then rebounds off the bank onto the rink it is also still in play if it is within the confines of the rink and at least 14m from the front of the mat. A bowl that has not touched the jack and rebounds onto the green is deemed to be dead and must be removed from the rink, preferably before it can come into contact with any live bowls.

## Displaced Bowls and Jacks

If such a non-toucher does rebound and displaces a live bowl, then that live bowl must be restored as near as possible to its original position. This action is undertaken by the opponent (or one of the opponents) of the player whose bowl has rebounded onto the green.

If bowls and jacks are displaced or interfered with by a player whilst they are in motion, or at rest, this can result in various courses of action being

Scotland's Colin Mitchell overseeing the 'head' during the British Isles Team Championships.
(Courtesy of Bowls International)

undertaken. The action taken is dictated by the skip of the opposing side to the player who interfered with a live bowl or jack. The skip's options include:

- restoring the displaced bowl or jack as near to its original position as possible;
- leaving the displaced bowl or jack where it rests;
- declaring the end dead and replaying it;
- declaring the affected bowl dead.

The above options largely apply to the various situations that may be experienced, but you will need to familiarize yourself with the exact Laws of the Sport relating to displaced bowls and jacks, since the specific circumstances involved dictate precisely which options can be considered.

### Ends

When the players have delivered all their bowls in one direction down the rink, this constitutes an 'end' played. Playing all their bowls back up the rink in the opposite direction constitutes another 'end'.

During each end players bowl alternately until all the bowls are delivered. Whoever wins the end – whoever's bowl(s) are closest to the jack after all the bowls are delivered – has the choice of delivering the jack on the next end or giving it to his opponent. The latter tactic gives the winner of the end the advantage of delivering the last bowl on the next end, which can be played in the knowledge that his opponent cannot reply. We will deal with the pros and cons of this later.

## Scoring and Duration of Games

At each end the objective is to get as many of your bowls closer to the jack than your opponent. For each of your bowls that is closer to the jack at the conclusion of any 'end', you will score a 'shot' (see Fig 4). At the conclusion of the

end the shots scored are recorded on a scorecard (for examples see Fig 5).

The duration of a bowls game is normally determined by the number of ends played – pairs (normally 21 ends), triples (normally 18 ends) and fours (normally 21 ends). In singles it usually does not matter how many ends are played, as the game is won by the player who first reaches 21 shots. Variations do occur in relation to domestic rules of play.

## Etiquette

The game of bowls is remarkable for its high standard of behaviour and sportsmanship. Many unwritten laws have been carried down through the generations, resulting in an etiquette for the game that is second to none. These may be summarized as follows:

- Always shake hands with your opponent(s) before and after the game.
- Be respectful of the playing surface. Do not drop your bowls on the green. Do not mark the green with badly delivered bowls and enter and leave the green by the steps/access provided.
- Stand still when a player is about to bowl and don't distract him while he is bowling.
- Remain behind the mat when a player is about to play.
- Stay on your rink and support your team. Concentrate on your own game – don't wander off or be distracted by other games.
- If you follow your bowl up the green make sure you are behind the head, and standing still, before the next player delivers his bowl.
- Stand well back from the head when a player is delivering his bowl. Be particularly alert when there is a heavy shot being played so that you do not interfere with any displaced bowls.
- Do not remove any bowls from the head until the outcome of the end has been agreed.
- Encourage your own players and 'shout on' your own team's bowls, but refrain from 'shouting through' your

opponents' bowls (willing them to miss) and from overtly revelling in any misfortune they may have. You may, of course, gloat inwardly as much as you want!
- If an umpire is called to measure, retire well away from the head until he has given his decision.
- Remember that when a bowler is on the mat it is his teammates who have control of the head. Do not stand between your opponents and the head when this is the case.
- Keep your shadow off the jack.
- Do not stand in a position where you obscure the rink boundary markers, as many bowlers use these as aiming points.
- Always dress correctly for all games.

## Coaching Help

All the countries in the United Kingdom have large coaching organizations that can offer help to get you started or a comprehensive range of services to assist you, whatever level of bowler you may be.

Some experienced individuals appear to think that if you admit you need 'coaching', then it infers you are not very good. This is absolute nonsense. The very good are the first to seek help if something is not working well. So if you don't like the idea of asking for coaching, why not ask for a little help?

## English Bowls Coaching Scheme

The English Bowls Coaching Scheme (EBCS) is a large organization with many thousands of coaches represented in all the different bowls codes: Flat Green, Crown Green, Federation and Short Mat.

Beginners' courses in the basics of the game run by the EBCS make it possible, within only four to six two-hour sessions, to learn enough knowledge and basic skills to allow you to play with your new friends and club colleagues in an enjoyable manner without fear of embarrassing yourself in any way.

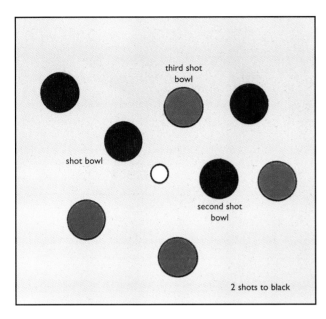
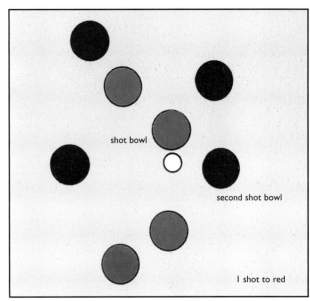

Fig 4  Examples of 'shot' bowls.

*2 shots to black* (right of left diagram)

*1 shot to red* (right of right diagram)

Labels on diagrams: third shot bowl, shot bowl, second shot bowl (left); shot bowl, second shot bowl (right)

---

**Left card:**

| Cumbria | versus | Durham |
|---|---|---|

Competition **MIDDLETON CUP**  Date **28/7/07**  Rink No. **4**

| LEAD | name |
| 2nd | name |
| 3rd | name |
| SKIP | name |

| LEAD | name |
| 2nd | name |
| 3rd | name |
| SKIP | name |

| END | SHOTS | TOTAL | END | SHOTS | TOTAL |
|---|---|---|---|---|---|
| 1 | 1 | 1 | 17 | | |
| 2 | 2 | 3 | 18 | | |
| 3 | — | 3 | 19 | | |
| 4 | — | 3 | 20 | | |
| 5 | 3 | 6 | 21 | | |
| 6 | — | 6 | 22 | | |
| 7 | | | 23 | | |
| 8 | | | 24 | | |
| 9 | | | 25 | | |
| 10 | | | 26 | | |
| 11 | | | 27 | | |
| 12 | | | 28 | | |
| 13 | | | 29 | | |
| 14 | | | 30 | | |
| 15 | | | 31 | | |
| 16 | | | SCORE | | |

| END | SHOTS | TOTAL | END | SHOTS | TOTAL |
|---|---|---|---|---|---|
| 1 | — | — | 17 | | |
| 2 | — | — | 18 | | |
| 3 | 1 | 1 | 19 | | |
| 4 | 4 | 5 | 20 | | |
| 5 | — | 5 | 21 | | |
| 6 | 1 | 6 | 22 | | |
| 7 | | | 23 | | |
| 8 | | | 24 | | |
| 9 | | | 25 | | |
| 10 | | | 26 | | |
| 11 | | | 27 | | |
| 12 | | | 28 | | |
| 13 | | | 29 | | |
| 14 | | | 30 | | |
| 15 | | | 31 | | |
| 16 | | | SCORE | | |

**Right card:**

Cumbria County Bowling Association (E.B.A.)

**WIGTON** VERSUS **SILLOTH**
PLAYED AT **Wigton**
RINK No. **3**  DATE **22/6/07**

| name | | name |
| name | | name |
| name | | name |
| name | | name |

| SHOTS | TOTAL | ENDS | SHOTS | TOTAL |
|---|---|---|---|---|
| 3 | 3 | 1 | — | — |
| 1 | 4 | 2 | — | — |
| 1 | 5 | 3 | — | — |
| — | 5 | 4 | 1 | 1 |
| 6 | 11 | 5 | — | 1 |
| — | 11 | 6 | 2 | 3 |
| | | 7 | | |
| | | 8 | | |
| | | 9 | | |
| | | 10 | | |
| | | 11 | | |
| | | 12 | | |
| | | 13 | | |
| | | 14 | | |
| | | 15 | | |
| | | 16 | | |
| | | 17 | | |
| | | 18 | | |
| | | 19 | | |
| | | 20 | | |
| | | 21 | | |

Total _____    Total _____

Fig 5  Examples of typical score cards.

*EBCS Northern Region Coach, Brian Warren, advising on the grip.*
(© Brian Warren)

An excellent scheme has also been developed specifically to enable, and encourage, children and young people to participate in our sport. Look for details of this initiative – the English Bowls Youth Development Scheme – on its website at www.eiba.co.uk/Young-People-Sport/ebyds.htm.

Your local club is also likely to have coaches within its membership and you simply need to ask them. Many clubs have specific times allocated to helping beginners or anyone with coaching needs, and these are normally advertised on the notice board.

The first move is up to you. All you have to do is ring someone, call in to a club, send an email or a short note and you will get information and help.

## Bowls and the Disabled Bowler

Bowls is unique among the popularly played sports in that it is completely 'open': the sport can be, and is, played between able-bodied bowlers and disabled bowlers. It is very common for disabled bowlers to be playing in their clubs, accepted as bowlers and treated on merit.

Several established associations exist to help and advise disabled bowlers; they also arrange national championships, competitions, matches and training.

**British Wheelchair Bowls Association**
(for bowlers who need to use a wheelchair to bowl)
Chairman: Ian Blackmore
Tel: 07932 791519
email: ianblackmore@bwba.org.uk
web: www.bwba.org.uk

**British Amputee and Les Autres Bowling Association**
(for amputee bowlers and others whose disability does not fit with the other associations)
BALASA & EBCS Coach: Ray Smith
Tel: 01543 573528

Such knowledge also pleases the green keeper of your club, because there is less danger of new bowlers damaging the green once they have been taught how to avoid it.

More experienced bowlers can get help with delivery problems of any type. In addition the EBCS runs courses for club bowlers seeking more knowledge and skill training in areas such as reading heads, playing with weight and positional woods.

Whatever help you believe you may need to improve your game and increase your enjoyment, a qualified coach can devise and adapt a plan to help you achieve that.

Coaching is also available for blind and partially sighted people, and for those with infirmities or confined to a wheelchair.

The EBCS grades its coaches at various licence qualification levels, but you don't need to worry about that. If you make contact they will work out how they can help: all they need from you is your cooperation and willingness to learn.

Don't let cost worry you, either. Because they volunteer their services, any charge they might make will be very small in comparison with any other sport.

The County Handbook produced for each code is likely to have the name and address details of the county coach. If you phone the person named, they will make contacts for you or give you details of whom to contact.

Alternatively you may leave a message at www.englishbowlscoaching.com, giving your name, address and telephone number, if that is the way you wish to be contacted. The officers' names, addresses and telephone numbers are on the site and any of them will be happy to help you.

### Cerebral Palsy Sport
(for bowlers with cerebral palsy, strokes or heart attacks)
Margaret Smith, Tel: 0115 9404 609

### English National Association of Visually Handicapped Bowlers
(for visually impaired bowlers)
web: www.englishblindbowls.co.uk

### Disability Bowls England
(for all bowlers with a disability in England)
President: Ian Blackmore
Tel: 07932 791519

DBE is an umbrella group, formally launched in February 2005, created to act as a focal point for bowlers with a disability in England. It has been designed to fill in the gaps of structure and funding that existed between the established associations representing bowlers with specific disabilities. DBE also acts as the link with the world governing body for bowlers with a disability.

Bowls clubs too can benefit from the advice available directly from the associations, particularly if they are concerned about how the Disability Discrimination Act might affect them. Alternatively, their National Governing Body might point them in the right direction: the British Wheelchair Bowls Association, for example, has very close links with, in particular, Bowls England and the EIBA on the subject of disabled access.

The most important thing to remember, though, is that disability need not be a bar to playing bowls or returning to the sport. If in doubt, just get in touch with the contacts listed above.

*Wheelchair bowlers playing indoor bowls.*
(Courtesy of Bowls International)

*David Gourlay has topped the WBT's World Ranking List with regularity and is a consistently high performer in televised events.*
*(Courtesy of Bowls International)*

# CHAPTER 3

# CHOOSING YOUR EQUIPMENT

## Bowls

A set of bowls is the most important item on your list of requirements. Selecting a set that is the correct size and weight to suit your hand, and the playing conditions you will encounter, is one of the most important decisions you will have to make in your bowling career.

The modern day bowl is made of plastic, moulded from a resin phenol-formaldehyde powder. Originally all bowls were manufactured from lignum vitae, the heaviest timber on earth, and many bowlers still refer to bowls as 'woods' as a consequence.

All bowls bend to a greater or lesser degree, but contrary to uninformed opinion the bowl is not 'weighted'. The 'bias' of a bowl is produced by precision machining, which creates the individual

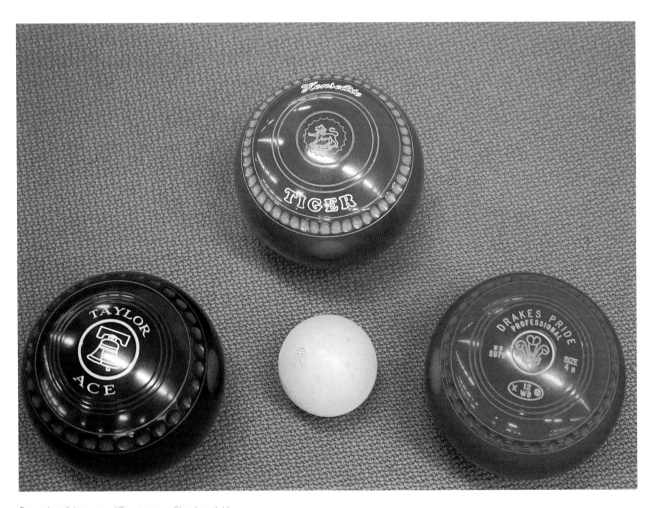

*Examples of the many different types of bowl available.*
(© Paul Walker)

*The larger ring (left) indicates the outside of the bowl, while the inside (right) has the small ring and technical information. The bowl will always bend towards its inside. The little ring should always be on the inside of the drawing line.*
*(© Paul Walker)*

*The official stamp on a bowl provides essential information about its origins. The markings here show that it is in accordance with World Bowls rules (WB), the manufacturer/tester may be identified by a letter code (A), the numerals denote the year of expiry, and the letter R indicates that the stamp is a registered trade mark.*
*(© Paul Walker)*

shape of the bowl. This dictates how much the bowl will curve on its path down the green. There are wide running bowls and narrow running bowls, with many variations in between. The curved path taken is always towards the inside of the bowl – the side with the smaller ring engraved in it.

The bowl bends in proportion to the speed it is travelling. It will only bend when the bowl begins to slow down. The point at which the bowl begins to turn, known as the 'shoulder', varies according to the distance between mat and jack (see Fig 6). The 'shoulder' is roughly two-thirds of the distance the bowl needs to run to its intended 'target'.

Bowls are made in identical sets of four. In all games each player must play with the appropriate number of bowls from the same set. All bowls must comply with the minimum bias of the World Bowls Governing Body's 'Master Bowl'. Every set of bowls is tested against this bowl and, having demonstrated they bend as much, or more than, the 'master bowl', the sets of bowls duly receive a 'stamp' of approval to signify that they are legitimate for play.

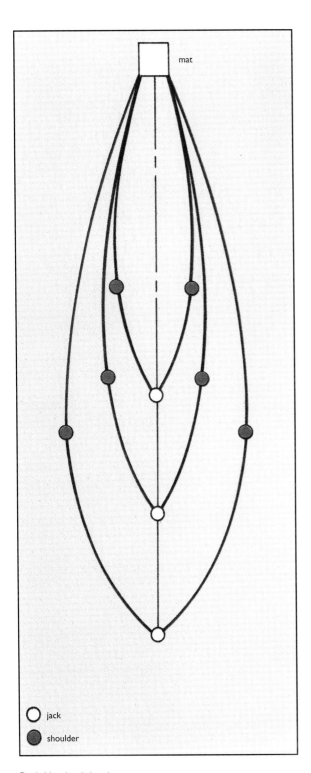

jack

shoulder

*Fig 6  How bowls bend.*

## Selecting the Right Set of Bowls for You

Bowls vary in size, weight, colour and design. There are eight different sizes of bowl, all varying in weight.

| (mm) | Bowl Size | (inches) |
|------|-----------|----------|
| 116 | 00 | 4⁹⁄₁₆ |
| 117 | 0 | 4⅝ |
| 121 | 1 | 4¾ |
| 122 | 2 | 4¹³⁄₁₆ |
| 124 | 3 | 4⅞ |
| 125 | 4 | 4¹⁵⁄₁₆ |
| 127 | 5 | 5 |
| 129 | 6 | 5¹⁄₁₆ |

It is essential that you choose a bowl that, first and foremost, suits the size of your hand. You must also choose one that can best perform on the surfaces on which you intend to play. You are strongly advised to seek the advice and assistance of a qualified coach and/or an experienced and respected bowler within the club you join. Don't fall into the trap of being tempted to buy a set of bowls because they are cheap and instantly available. You must spend valuable time trying a variety of sizes and 'biases' until you are totally happy with a chosen set.

## Selecting the Correct Size of Bowl

Whatever bowl you choose in terms of its bending capabilities, it is absolutely essential that your bowl is comfortable in your hand. It must not be too small or too big. If it is too big it will cause tension in your hand. If it is too small it will result in 'over gripping'. Both situations will cause subsequent delivery problems.

Two standard practices are used to ensure you have the correct size of bowl.

**Method 1** Take the bowl and place both hands around the widest part. Extend your thumb and middle finger. These should touch, but only just.

*One method used to determine the correct size of bowl – touching thumbs and middle fingers.*
*(© Paul Walker)*

*Another useful test to determine the correct size of bowl – turning the bowl over in an outstretched hand.*
*(© Paul Walker)*

This test should not be used in isolation, however, and a second method, strongly advocated by Jimmy Davidson, a former National Coach, should be applied as a more definitive measure of the suitability of the size.

**Method 2** Pick up a bowl with your three middle fingers placed along the running surface of the bowl, and then extend your arm out in front at shoulder level. Your hand will be on top of the bowl. Then twist your wrist in a circular motion so that the bowl is now on top of the hand. If you can undertake these actions without the bowl slipping or dropping out of your hand then the bowl is not too big for you.

The critical point in the delivery action, as far as the size of bowl is concerned, is the top of the back swing. The bowl will be safe for you to use if you can rotate the wrists, as described above, at this point.

## Further Considerations

I cannot overemphasize the importance of the bowl being comfortable in your hand. It must 'feel' good. Your set of bowls should be your 'prized possession', which gives you a sense of pride, and confidence, while you are playing.

The type of bowl you choose, however, will also need to respond well to the playing conditions involved. Outdoor play generally involves slow running greens. For these a medium bias bowl will be required. For indoor surfaces and quicker outdoor surfaces (as found in Australia and New Zealand, in particular) a narrower biased bowl will serve you well. The theory behind this is simple – the narrower bowl gives you a shorter route to the jack with less margin for error. If you miss the line with a wide-running bowl on a quick surface it will deviate across and away from the centre line more than a narrow-biased bowl. Equally it is harder to match the correct line to the required length with a wide running bowl than a narrow one.

The position you play is also a key influence on your choice of bowl. If you

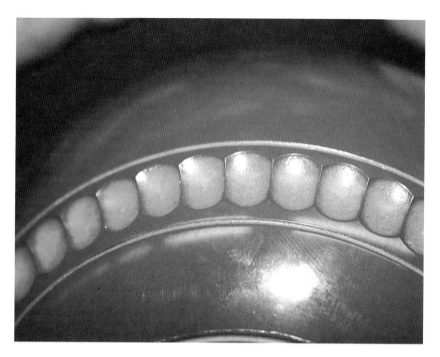

*TOP, ABOVE & TOP RIGHT: Examples of types of grip available.*
*(© Paul Walker)*

lead, or even play second, then you can choose to play with a narrower biased bowl even outdoors. You have a clear route to the jack and you will be largely playing the draw shot throughout your games. If you are playing at the back end of rinks, pairs or triples combinations, you will be playing a variety of shots and you will not normally have the luxury of a clear path to the jack. You will invariably have to draw and run around bowls. A bending bowl is a distinct advantage in these circumstances.

## Bowls with Grips

You can also buy bowls that have 'grips' machined into their design. They may consist of sets of 'dimples' or 'serrations' around the outside edges of the bowl.

These are designed to provide a better grip, particularly in cold and wet weather conditions. There is no definitive judgement as to their effectiveness. Many bowlers prefer them and strongly applaud the benefits they bring. You must test them out for yourself. If you feel that bowls with grips are beneficial to you, from either a practical or psychological perspective, then use them.

## Coloured Bowls

There is now a wide range of coloured bowls readily available. While they are more expensive than the traditional black and brown sets, there is no doubt they are becoming increasingly popular. There is no technical advantage in playing with coloured bowls apart from the fact that you can easily identify where your bowls are positioned on the rink. Equally it is just as easy for your opponent to see them too. It is almost entirely an aesthetic consideration. If a particular coloured set of bowls gives you that 'feel good' factor and adds to your enjoyment of the game then go for it. Beauty is in the eye of the beholder, as they say, and Mark Walton's bright pink set of bowls won the English Bowling Association national singles title at Worthing in 2006!

*Coloured bowls contrasting with the traditional black. Many colours are now available.*
(© Paul Walker)

## Final Decision

Whatever bowl you choose will be your individual decision. I would, however, strongly advise you to digest the above information and try a variety of bowls before you settle on your final choice. There will be plenty of different types at the club where you will be playing and plenty of members, not least the club coach, to help with your deliberation. Don't forget, the bowl that serves you well outdoors might not be ideal for your indoor play. Importantly, too, don't fall into the trap of buying a set because they are on offer or cheap – they may be totally unsuitable for your style of play. Be sure to test out your options thoroughly before making a decision. Ensure you give yourself the best possible start by acquiring a set of bowls in which you have full confidence and that gives you the important psychological advantage of knowing you have the best 'tools' for the job.

# Clothing and Footwear

You will spend many hours on greens with varying conditions underfoot and in all sorts of weather conditions. Unlike those in the southern hemisphere, we continue to play through rain, whether it be intermittent or continuous. We only evacuate the green when it becomes flooded.

It naturally follows that a good quality set of waterproofs and a pair of comfortable watertight shoes should be on your essential list of requirements.

## Waterproofs

Ensure that your waterproofs are genuinely 'waterproof' and not just showerproof. You could find yourself on the green for two or three hours in continual rain. The normal colour is white.

## Shoes

Shoes must be smooth-soled and heel-less. Ensure you don't buy shoes designed for indoor play (those with aeration holes to cool the foot) and then play outside in them when it rains. You will probably have the choice of white, grey and brown shoes. Certain competitions, clubs and associations have regulations governing the use of certain coloured footwear. World Bowls and National Authorities reserve the right to allow the use of specific colours of footwear. The most universally popular coloured shoe is now white. The design and quality of footwear has been improving by the year and there is now an excellent choice of shoes to suit all tastes and pockets. Don't forget that long hours on the green in all day and weekend play merits the use of a good quality, comfortable shoe. Choose one that will protect and support your feet, and enhance your enjoyment and performance during your games. Remember the old adage – you just get what you pay for.

## Clothing

Dress regulations for bowlers vary in the UK and across the world. Traditionally, the dress that has been associated with flat green bowls has been quite rigid. Most clubs still require at least grey trousers or skirts with white or cream attire above the waist.

Coloured club/county shirts have started to become more popular and are certainly brightening up the game. This has followed the lead of televised bowls tournaments, in which the players have matching coloured shirts and bowls. Each club has its own dress code, whilst the national competitions and county matchplay also have their dress requirements. The latter and the final stages of the national competitions require white trousers and white tops (or the appropriate approved coloured top if applicable).

*A selection of modern, quality footwear.*
*(© Paul Walker)*

*Typical clothing attire for club play, as seen at the Cumbria Indoor Bowls Club.*
*(© Paul Walker)*

*A colourful spectacle as England play Wales in the British Isles Team Championships.*
*(Courtesy of Bowls International)*

You need to find out about the dress code you will be required to conform to, and then acquire the appropriate articles of clothing you need. There is a large choice of clothing easily available from both high street stores and bowls equipment suppliers, which you will be able to find out about through the club you join. A wide selection of windproof light jackets, pullovers, sweaters and various types of shirt will help you combat all the elements during outdoor play and again maximize your enjoyment. Ensure that anything you wear is not too small or tight fitting. You must not wear anything that can inhibit your desired delivery style: a sleeve that is pulling too tightly under the arm or around the wrist when you deliver a bowl will adversely affect your performance.

*Norfolk play Bucks in the semi-final of the 2006 Middleton Cup County Championship.*
*(Courtesy of Bowls International)*

*Two good multi-purpose bowls bags showing attractive features: mobility, good zips, multi compartments and self-contained bowls carriers (2 × 2 bowls).*
*(© Paul Walker)*

# Other Necessary Accessories

You have now identified the bowls, clothing and shoes you will need to play bowls. There are still a few more accessories that you will need.

## Bowls Bag

Like bowls shoes, bag design has been modified and improved over recent years. You need a good bag to convey your bowls and equipment to your matches. There are many types to select from. The price varies according to their quality. Durability, mobility, capacity and special features are all factors in determining which are the most suitable. Again the choice is yours. The look of the bag, ease of access to its various spaces – a good zip that opens and closes efficiently around the bowls compartment is always a welcome feature – and its mobility are all elements that you might wish to consider. The presence of a shoulder strap and the ability to pull the bag on a set of wheels make life a lot easier when your bag has to be carried excessive distances. Ensure you make life easy for yourself by selecting a bag that gives quick access to your equipment and one that can be moved without too much effort. Look for the bag that has all the features that suits your needs and aspirations.

## Duster

A duster/cloth is another essential piece of equipment. Always have a duster with you. A sudden shower, moisture in the grass, even sweaty hands – these can all leave your bowl wet and slippery. As you need complete control of your bowl you need to make sure it is dried off before each delivery. A good chamois leather is often used for this purpose.

## Gripping Agents

It is also wise to possess a gripping agent to smear onto your bowls if they become difficult to grip properly. This can happen after they become wet and dried off. I find it very useful to apply a gripping agent, such as waxes and gels that are readily available at little cost. Frequent play indoors can make your bowl over-polished and in need of the same treatment.

## Gloves

The use of bowling gloves is also becoming more popular. These are very similar to golf gloves and are used to assist with getting a better grip of the bowl. When used outside they overcome another common problem, keeping your hands warm on cold days. (Many ladies use hand warmers and you may find it useful to include this on your equipment list.) Gloves might not suit everyone, but again if you think they might help you then try them out. You will soon see if they are of benefit or not.

## Measure

It is also useful to possess a bowls measure. This is used when the shot cannot be decided by the naked eye. You will definitely need one if you are playing in the third position – it is normally the third's job to measure on behalf of his skip. There is a good choice of inexpensive measures available from bowls equipment companies.

A bowls glove.
(© Brian Warren)

# PART 2

# SKILLS AND
# TECHNIQUES

CHAPTER 4

# GRIP AND DELIVERY –
# THE ABSOLUTE ESSENTIALS

Your grip and delivery technique are the two elements that most influence performance. It is absolutely essential that you develop and adopt a comfortable, efficient and effective means of delivering the bowl. In this way you will give it the maximum chance of achieving the correct line and length needed to fulfil its purpose.

We shall look at all the relevant components in detail – grip, stance, head position, step and follow through – to ensure you are fully aware of the basic requirements. You can then practise, and practise, until you 'groove' in an action that is both comfortable and effective for your individual purpose.

## Grip

There are basically two types of grip: the Cradle Grip and the Claw Grip. There are other variations in between, but it is

*ABOVE & BELOW: Cradle grip.*
*(© Paul Walker)*

---

**KEY POINT**

1. Whatever grip you choose, it is essential that the middle fingers are spread evenly and comfortably across the running surface of the bowl and ideally are parallel to it.
2. Ensure your grip results in the smooth delivery of the bowl onto the playing surface. Ideally you should consult a qualified coach at this crucial stage. It is essential that your grip is effective from the very start of your tuition. You could develop an excellent delivery style, as described later in this section, that would be totally wasted if your grip was wrong and resulted in wobbled bowls.

ABOVE & BELOW: *Claw grip.*
(© Paul Walker)

prudent at the introductory stage to concentrate on a choice between these two.

The key factors in determining that choice will be:

(i) making sure the bowl is comfortable in your hand
  • avoiding over-gripping so that the hand and fingers are not too tense;
  • ensuring the fingers are not overstretched.

(ii) ensuring that the bowl 'feels' right in your hand. You should and will develop your own instinctive feel that this is so.

## Cradle Grip

This is a simple and comfortable grip and is in widespread use in the UK. The bowl rests in the palm of the hand with the fingers simply cupping the bowl, not gripping it. The thumb provides the steadying influence on the side of the bowl.

This grip allows flexibility with the choice of bowls, as it compensates for physical weakness and for a small hand. The cradle grip enables a larger bowl to be used if desired, though great care should be taken not to be over-ambitious in using a bowl that is too big for hand and finger size.

## Claw Grip

This grip is also very popular in the UK and is very versatile in coping with both slow and quicker surfaces. The fingers and thumb play a much more significant part in this grip compared to the cradle grip. There is little or no contact with the palm of the hand. The weight of the bowl is distributed through the fingers, which are extended along the running surface in parallel fashion. The thumb completes the grip by resting on, or near, the large outer ring of the bowl.

## USEFUL CHECKS

### AVOIDING A WOBBLE

Choosing and engaging a suitable grip for your individual circumstances is one of the initial key stages in ensuring you are in complete control of the bowl when it leaves your hand and that you achieve a smooth delivery.

While developing and refining your delivery you may find that the bowl has a slight wobble when it is released from your hand. This invariably means that your grip is still not quite right and needs some minor adjustment.

**Check 1** Hold the bowl out with your arm at full extension. Grip the bowl as you normally do. If the bowl is not perfectly upright you will probably need to change your grip.

**Check 2** Look at the position of your thumb. Sometimes the thumb can be stretched too far around the top of the bowl, resulting in over-gripping the bowl. This causes a strain on the hand, particularly in the groove between the thumb and the index finger. Dropping the thumb to a more comfortable position on the larger outer rings around the disc produces a much more comfortable and effective grip, which should eradicate any unwanted wobble.

*Thumb positioned too high on the bowl.*
*(© Paul Walker)*

The thumb can also be held too low down when employing the cradle grip. This results in the little finger playing an unwanted part during the release of the bowl – as the last part of the hand to touch the bowl it exerts enough pressure to cause a wobble.

**Check 3** Be watchful where you put your little finger. You must ensure it does not creep too far up the side of the bowl, particularly with the claw grip. If it does it can similarly cause unwanted pressure on the side of the bowl and cause a wobble. You must try and keep it underneath the bowl.

*Good alignment of the middle fingers along the running surface of the bowl.*
*(© Paul Walker)*

*Correct placement of the little finger.*
*(© Paul Walker)*

*Perfect alignment of fingers on the running surface.*
*(© Paul Walker)*

*Incorrect placement of the little finger.*
*(© Paul Walker)*

**Check 4** Make sure that the middle finger is aligned on the running surface of the bowl and not significantly away from it. The last point of contact on the bowl at delivery should be with the tip of the middle finger. If this last dominant push from the middle finger is not at the running surface it will cause a wobble.

*Incorrect alignment of fingers on the running surface.*
*(© Paul Walker)*

# Delivery

The development of an effective delivery action is the next fundamental task that must be mastered. You will be looking to adopt a well-balanced and free-flowing action, and one which is economical in terms of eliminating unnecessary movement. Above all you must achieve a high degree of consistency. You will not

*Richard Corsie* MBE *– a naturally gifted player – was three times World Indoor Singles Champion (four times a finalist) and Commonwealth Games Singles Gold Medalist, and had one of the smoother and more effortless deliveries in the game.*
*(© Paul Walker)*

achieve satisfactory performances or results on a regular basis if you continually vary any of the key elements of your delivery.

We will be looking in detail at the recognized 'good practice' principles associated with all the components of the delivery action. Any good coach or instructor, however, will tell you that these should not be regarded as 'cardinal rules' that must be followed to the letter. It is much more effective to look at the bowler's natural action and shape an effective style to suit their particular physique and personality.

That is why you will invariably find that the very first request by a coach to his pupil is for him to stand on the mat and deliver a jack without any prior instruction. From there the necessary adjustments and choice of stance can be made and practised until the required consistency is achieved.

Now let us look in detail at the actions involved with a good delivery. First, it is important to appreciate that delivery is not one distinct action. It embraces everything you do from the moment you step onto the mat until you have delivered the bowl, including your follow-through action.

## Individual Styles

As was touched on above, it is important to remember that the stance and style you adopt is one of personal preference. Over your formative period of practice and play you will gradually adjust your delivery action and stance to what is totally comfortable for you. There is scope within the good practice framework to allow you to incorporate your own natural attributes and movements into your delivery action. My good friend Jimmy Davidson, a true visionary in the world of bowls coaching and administration but sadly no longer with us, always used to say, 'a person's delivery is as unique as a fingerprint'. He also believed that if everything is 'right' at the precise moment the bowl leaves the hand, then everything that has happened before has been right, including any idiosyncrasies of the delivery action and the grip.

It is not always the best-looking style that provides the top-quality shot. Some of the best bowlers in the game have delivery actions that certainly wouldn't fit any textbook. The crucial factor is indeed how a bowl leaves your hand – it must roll smoothly away along its running surface. Any 'bump' or 'wobble' will usually detract from it achieving the line and length intended.

So let's look at the best guidelines that can assist you to produce a smooth and consistent delivery.

# Stance

## Position of the Feet

It may seem that it is the most natural thing to stand with your feet touching each other in order to make sure they are within the confines of the mat. You must resist the temptation, however, and ensure that your feet are slightly apart. This provides you with a much firmer base on which to start and gives you a better balance to aid the rest of your delivery actions.

A good starting point is to stand on the middle of the mat with your feet parallel, a few inches apart and pointing along the line

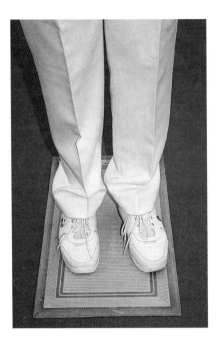

*Positioning of the feet on the mat is partly a matter of individual preference. Keep your feet slightly apart, and angled towards the line of delivery. When you step out with your lead foot it will dictate the line your bowl will take. You must make sure your stance and step enable you to deliver down that correct line.*
(© Paul Walker)

ABOVE & BELOW: *Forehand.*
(© Paul Walker)

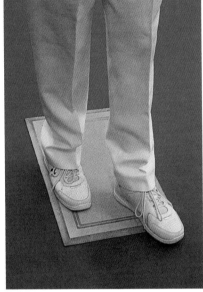

ABOVE & BELOW: *Backhand.*
(© Paul Walker)

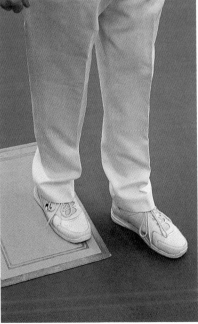

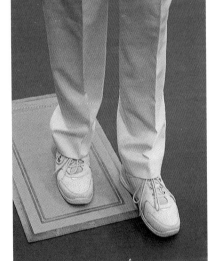

*Drive.*
(© Paul Walker)

that you intend to deliver your bowl. However, there are a number of variations that are perfectly acceptable. It is up to you which stance you find most comfortable and effective in achieving a smooth step forward and accurate delivery line.

At the moment of delivery, when the bowl touches the surface of play, make sure your back foot is either on the mat or directly above it.

## Bend Your Knees

Whatever stance you adopt (see below), you need to ensure that your action delivers the bowl smoothly onto the surface. To do this your delivery hand must reach low enough to be at surface level when the bowl is released. In order to achieve this important objective you must bend your knees accordingly.

You do not need a bowl to test your success in getting down low enough. Practise your action by just brushing the grass, or even the carpet if you wish to do it at home. If your fingertips are not touching the surface you are not low enough, and you need to bend your knees more.

ABOVE & BELOW: *Good examples of how the knees must be bent to achieve a smooth delivery.* (© Paul Walker)

## Most Common Stances

Despite all that has been said about the scope for bowlers to demonstrate individualistic characteristics, it is still rare to see a reasonably accomplished bowler whose delivery action does not largely conform to one of the stances described below. Whichever of these you adopt and develop for your own purposes, it must become second nature to you. So let's have a look at what might suit your requirements.

### Athletic (or Upright) Stance

This is undoubtedly the most popular stance used throughout the world. It is simple and the most natural. It also has a distinct advantage on the slower greens of the northern hemisphere, since it enables you to impart more force behind the bowl and still maintain the accuracy required. It is also suited to all shots, particularly the weighted ones, as it allows you to get the entire momentum of your body behind the shot.

### Crouch Stance

This stance has been immortalized by David Bryant, the English bowls legend and multi-championship winner. The full crouch has the legs fully bent with the entire bodyweight taken on the back of

The athletic stance demonstrated by England International Stuart Airey, one of the best Number 2 players in the British Isles.
(© Paul Walker)

Robert Weale, who has won both World Indoor Singles and World Outdoor Fours titles, is one of the few top bowlers to use the crouch stance.
(Courtesy of Bowls International)

the legs. As you would expect, this stance is very demanding even if you are fully fit. If you are overweight and/or have problems with your knees, the physical demands of moving up from the full crouch position to the final point of delivery can prove to be excessive and create too many problems in terms of affecting balance and comfort.

Whilst there is no doubt it worked impeccably for David Bryant, and is still very effective for Robert Weale, I feel the extra pressure on the legs and the upward movement involved (from squatting to delivery) are added complications. They can cause unnecessary problems, which can be avoided with the alternative variations of the upright stance.

## Semi-Crouch Stance

Whilst it is termed 'semi-crouch', this stance is in reality a variation of the 'athletic'. Instead of adopting a fully upright position, you may find it more practical to bend both your knees and body so that you are in a lower position. Being closer to the ground, and a stage nearer the final delivery action, you are actually reducing

*England's Andy Thomson using his own variation of the semi-crouch stance.*
*(Courtesy of Bowls International)*

overall movement and minimizing the chance of error. This means that it is a more efficient form of stance. It is very extensively used and is totally flexible in terms of allowing the bowler to choose the most comfortable and appropriate position for their knees and back that suits their individual physique and natural technique. That said, care must be taken to ensure that you adopt exactly the same stance every time so that you can achieve the necessary consistency of delivery.

## Fixed Stance

As its name suggests, this stance eliminates the forward body movement associated with the upright and crouch stances, and dictates that the arm action is solely responsible for the delivery of the bowl.

*Prolific title winner, Margaret Johnston MBE, uses a classic semi-crouch stance.*
*(© Paul Walker)*

*Fixed stance.*
*(© Paul Walker)*

The lead foot must be set at a comfortable distance down the line of delivery. Your free hand is normally positioned on the thigh/knee of the outstretched leading leg in order to maintain the satisfactory balance and stability that is even more critical for this type of stance.

From a technical point of view this stance has a lot to commend it. It eliminates leg and body movement and the potential coordination problems associated with them. The fixed leg position also maximizes the selection of a good line. Take away the forward movement of the body, however, and you lose the natural momentum associated with it, leaving the movement of the arm as the sole means of propulsion. This can be a severe handicap on slow-running outdoor greens. It is perhaps for this reason that the fixed stance is not more commonly used.

## Clinic (or South African) Stance

Also known as the 'semi-fixed' stance, this was developed by Dr Julius Sergay. This South African bowler formed a 'clinic' of national champions to study and develop the techniques that would achieve success. The 'clinic' stance emerged from this process and has been used to great effect by South African bowlers, and many others, in international competition ever since.

It is achieved by standing on the mat facing the line of delivery and then taking a short step forward with your lead foot along the line of delivery. Your weight must be retained on your back foot. Your knees are normally slightly bent with your body inclined towards the delivery line. You now step forward again with your front foot to achieve the same comfortable distance as that associated with all other stances described above. Delivery now becomes the same as that undertaken with the athletic stance, with the same natural transfer of weight from the back foot to the front.

The clinic stance allows much more freedom of action than the fixed stance and shares its benefit of mapping out your desired line in advance.

*Clinic stance.*
(© Paul Walker)

# Delivering the Bowl

We have looked in detail at the grip and stance you can adopt. Applied correctly they will undoubtedly provide a solid foundation on which to develop an effective delivery action. This is the last, vital part of the 'mechanics' that have to be mastered if you are to perform proficiently and derive the maximum enjoyment from the game.

It is absolutely essential that your delivery action is free from basic error. It can be compared to a golf swing: if certain basics are not achieved you will never be able to play the game properly or derive the level of satisfaction from it you should. It is exactly the same with a bowler's delivery action. So what, in simple terms, should we be trying to achieve?

You are gripping the bowl in a comfortable way with your fingers running parallel with the running surface. You are standing on the mat, feet slightly apart, knees bent as much as you feel necessary. Your body is well balanced and relaxed.

You now need to swing your bowling arm backwards. As part of a pendulum motion, you step forward with your lead foot (left, if you are right-handed) along the line you intend to deliver. Now bring your bowling arm forward as your weight is transferred to your front foot. Your knees will now be bent to allow the bowl to be brought through and delivered at grass (surface) level with the fingers almost touching the surface at the point of delivery.

Now let's look at that in detail as we go through the full action. What are the key elements?

## 1 Single Action

Whilst there are a number of different components that make up your delivery, you must always consider and treat it as one single flowing action. All the movements involved – and the fewer the better – must be coordinated to produce a smooth and consistent delivery.

## 2 Balance and Freedom of Movement

Good body balance and freedom of movement (not too tense) are basic necessities. You will not achieve consistency or accurate delivery line if you can't maintain your balance or restrict your arm movement, which must be flowing, yet controlled, and certainly not jerky or tense.

## 3 Back Swing

The back swing is the first stage of the arm movement. It is timed to coincide with your step forward with your front foot. Some bowlers begin the back swing at the same time as they begin to step forward. Others delay their forward step until they have completed their back swing. It is down to what comes naturally when you go through your full delivery action. The back and forward swing,

*Controlled backswing coordinating with the step forward.*
(© Paul Walker)

together with the step forward, is however very much related to the simultaneous lowering of the body, which enables the delivery hand to get as close as possible to the bowling surface. If there is a significant gap between your bowl and the bowling surface when it is delivered it is a good indication that your knees are not sufficiently bent.

During the back swing your arm must not stray away from your body and the strength of your delivery is dictated by the length of the back swing. As you practise you will be able to mentally relate the distance you need to bowl with the amount of backswing that is required. Through dedicated practice and application this seemingly difficult equation will become second nature to you. It may not seem like it during your initial coaching clinics, but it will eventually click into place.

*ABOVE & RIGHT: Bowling arm kept close to the body.*
(© Paul Walker)

## 4 Forward Swing

In the case of the athletic delivery the forward swing is accompanied by the forward movement of the body, which is as much part of the motive force involved in propelling the bowl as the arm movement. The forward swing will also be accompanied by a step forward with the front foot. This must be no longer than your normal walking step, since any further will adversely affect your balance. This step must be directed down your intended delivery line, as the delivery hand will follow the front foot. If your feet are in the wrong position your hand will follow the wrong line.

With the fixed stance the forward step has been taken from the outset, so no further movement is necessary. You will find that the back swing is more limited with this delivery action and can be a disadvantage on heavy surfaces. It can, however, also be argued that the fixed stance ensures your leading leg is firmly set on the delivery line, and minimizes any deviation from that desired line during delivery.

ABOVE & BELOW: *Smooth forward swing along the delivery line, which is dictated by the position of the front foot.*
(© Paul Walker)

## USEFUL CHECKS

### HOW TO AVOID 'BUMPING' YOUR BOWL

This problem relates to a bowl that is not delivered at surface level. Instead it is launched somewhere above it and 'bumps' onto the playing surface. This generally has an adverse effect on the weight of the bowl (usually taking some running off it) and its intended line.

It can develop after many years of bowling. A bowler may have started off with a smooth, athletic delivery action, but after several years a slight bump on delivery will appear and then the bump gets worse. The problem stems from the fact that the knees are not bending as much as they used to years ago.

The cure is very simple: ensure the knees are bent a little further when you take up your stance on the mat. And make sure they remain in that lower position. You can practise your revised stance both at home and on the green. You will be able to experience an immediate improvement in your delivery.

### HOW TO AVOID 'HOOKING' YOUR BOWL

Another common problem that can arise is 'hooking' your bowling arm across your body. This usually happens on the forehand. Many bowlers agree that the 'backhand' is the more natural hand to bowl because the bowling arm feels closer to the body. On the forehand the arm is more isolated as it is thrust away from the body. In doing so it is all too easy for the elbow to move too far away from it, causing the arm to 'hook' across. This is particularly the case when the swing of the arm away from the body is obstructed by the hip. It is then natural for the swing to become a hooking motion around the hips rather than in a straight line along the intended line of delivery.

The solution lies in altering the position of your feet on the mat. You must turn your feet clockwise (assuming you are right-handed) so they are now in a position that moves your hip out of the way. Now, instead of the bowling arm being hooked around the hip, it can go forward close to the front of the body and in a straight line along the intended delivery line.

*ABOVE & LEFT: Fix your eyes on the delivery line. Two different stages of delivery are shown here, but the head remains still and the eyes are firmly fixed on the aiming point(s).*
*(© Paul Walker)*

## 5  Head Position

During the delivery action the head must remain still with the eyes fixed firmly on the aiming point(s) you are using to select your delivery line for the bowl. Your head must not be held too high, and you must try to avoid looking anywhere except at the jack or the line you intend to play (see Aiming Points below).

## 6  Alignment

From the moment you commence your backswing you must try to ensure your shoulder, elbow, forearm and hand are all in alignment. The elbow should never stray far from the body. A useful check for you to carry out is to freeze your delivery at the point when you are actually ready to release the bowl. The bowl in your hand should be in line with your back foot.

*ABOVE & RIGHT: Good alignment is necessary for a good delivery.*
(© Paul Walker)

*ABOVE & LEFT: The required smooth delivery is achieved by releasing the bowl at green level, and onto its full running surface.*
*(© Paul Walker)*

## 7 Release

The whole purpose of perfecting an effective delivery action is to give your bowl the best chance of achieving the successful line and length required for any particular shot you are playing. Releasing a bowl on line, at surface level and fully on its running surface will give it the perfect start.

## 8 Non-Bowling Arm

The non-bowling (or loose) arm also has a role to play in your delivery. It can be crucial in ensuring that you retain the necessary balance when the bowl is being released. Most bowlers place their loose arms on their thigh or knee. Some let it hang loose at their side. If this is the case you must try to ensure it is in exactly the same position during every delivery so that the necessary consistency is achieved.

The best position for your non-bowling arm.
(© Paul Walker)

An alternative position for your non-bowling arm.
(© Paul Walker)

# 9  Follow Through

On release of the bowl you must try to follow through with your arm along the delivery line, with your head remaining still and eyes on your bowl until it has completed its course.

# 10  Aiming Point(s)

There have been many references in this section to the 'delivery line'. This is the perceived line you think your bowl needs to take to achieve its objective. The line you have chosen will have mentally taken into account some key factors: the speed at which you intend to deliver the bowl (its 'weight'), the bias of your bowl (how much it bends), the distance to the jack or target area, and the nature of the playing surface, such as whether it is fast or slow. This analysis process will, believe it or not, become automatic as you gain more experience.

*ABOVE & BELOW: A decisive follow through along the delivery line increases your effectiveness, both for a drive (below) and for a draw (above).*
*(© Paul Walker)*

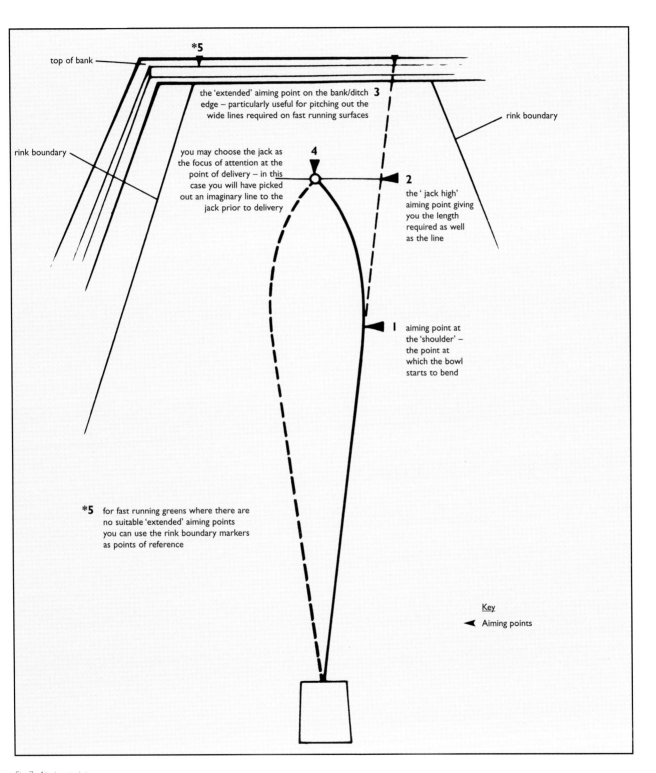

top of bank

*5

the 'extended' aiming point on the bank/ditch **3**
edge – particularly useful for pitching out the
wide lines required on fast running surfaces

rink boundary

rink boundary

you may choose the jack as
the focus of attention at the
point of delivery – in this
case you will have picked
out an imaginary line to the
jack prior to delivery

**4**

**2**

the ' jack high'
aiming point giving
you the length
required as well
as the line

**I**   aiming point at
the 'shoulder' –
the point at
which the bowl
starts to bend

*5   for fast running greens where there are
no suitable 'extended' aiming points
you can use the rink boundary markers
as points of reference

Key
◀ Aiming points

Fig 7  Aiming points.

Once you have decided on which line will be the most appropriate for the shot you are about to play, you need to fix it in your mind. To do this you are advised to pick out an 'aiming point' to focus on at the precise moment you deliver your bowl. You will also find that focusing on an aiming point assists in disciplining your delivery movements and helps in achieving consistency in your action.

What is the best aiming point to select? I refer again to coaching guru Jimmy Davidson, who always used to answer that question with 'Whatever works for you'. He is right. You must find the best option that you can clearly relate to, and test it to see if it can effectively guide you to your desired objective. So what options do you have? I think the majority of bowlers look for the 'shoulder' of your proposed delivery line. This is the point where your bowl begins to bend, usually about two-thirds of the way up the green. When you play outdoors you can usually pick out a blemish or particular patch of colour to home in on at this point, a method favoured by Tony Allcock, the multi-World Champion. Others, like the great David Bryant, will pick out a point on a bank related to the position of the rink marker. On greens with quicker surfaces, such as indoor greens, the hands have a much wider swing and an extended aiming point can be more effective in achieving the necessary wider bias. An aiming point level with the jack length is recommended by the South African coaching innovator Dr Julius Sergay. Using this point, he suggests, will enable you to feed in critical length without risking looking at the jack as you deliver, which may make you pull your bowl narrow.

I use a variation of this jack length strategy: I look firmly at the jack as I deliver the bowl, but I have selected a line in relation to it immediately prior to delivery. This method is also used by my international colleague Andy Thomson, who is a prolific title winner, including World Indoor and Outdoor Championships. This line is kept in your sphere of vision while focusing on the jack at the moment of delivery. If the object of the exercise is to get close to the jack, I believe it is best to focus your eye on that specific target. This will enable your eye to send precise information on distance and location to the brain, which then conditions the delivery action and dictates how well you achieve the required distance and speed.

Jimmy Davidson always favoured a distant aiming point. He argued that the more distant the aiming point, and the more you stare at it as you deliver, the more it helps to keep your head still. If you do that you receive a constant picture that assists you in coordinating the rest of your body movement with it. This principle is put to good use with my choice of aiming point as explained above.

You must, however, choose for yourself which aiming point you can use to the best effect. Try them all and see which one produces the best results (see Fig 7).

---

**KEY POINT**

Remember to keep your weight requirement in your mind while you are fixing your attention on your chosen aiming point. Keep your head still and that aiming point in your sight throughout your delivery action.

---

## Groove in Your Delivery Action

You are now ready to 'groove in' your delivery action. You are familiar with all the delivery guidelines. You know how to hold a bowl, where to stand and step, how to deliver and where to aim for.

You must now put all your new knowledge into purposeful practice. I cannot emphasize enough the need to produce a smooth, clean, flowing delivery. Your performance, success and enjoyment of the game depend on it. Practise, practise, practise, until you have developed a delivery style that you can utilize consistently and without thinking. Your ultimate aim is to be able to stand on the mat and concentrate on the shot you are about to play – not the mechanics of delivering your bowl.

---

**KEY POINT**

Don't forget that once the mat is moved and the length of the jack is altered you will have to find a new aiming point.

---

**PURPOSEFUL PRACTICE WITH A QUALIFIED COACH**

Make sure you take advantage of your national coaching scheme at this crucial stage of your development as a bowler. The English Bowls Coaching Scheme, along with those of the other national coaching bodies, has tried and tested exercises to help you develop the most appropriate delivery action to suit your physique and natural style. The basic initial practices include:

- Delivering jacks to various lengths;
- Delivering bowls down the forehand and backhand lines of the rink to familiarize yourself with the bias of the bowls and the lines required.

Coaches will also be well equipped to iron out delivery defects if they arise.

---

*OPPOSITE: Willie Wood MBE has been consistently successful over five decades of international bowls. He has played in seven Commonwealth Games and eight World Championships, all on varying surfaces worldwide, winning two Gold Medals from the former and three Golds from the latter. (Courtesy of Bowls International)*

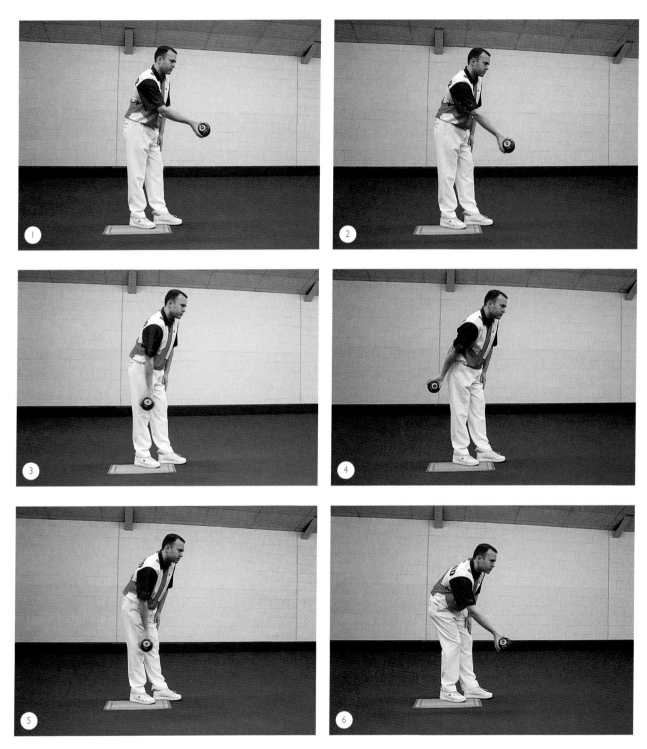

*Best practice sequence for a drawing delivery (side view), illustrating all the key elements (photographs 1–12).*
(© Paul Walker)

*Best practice sequence for a drawing delivery (front view), illustrating all the key elements (photographs 1–12, pp. 58–60).*
(© Paul Walker)

5

6

7

8

# PLAYING THE SHOTS

You should now be familiar and, it is to be hoped, proficient in the art of delivering a bowl. You will also have a basic understanding of what you are trying to achieve. Now let's look in detail at the various 'shots' you will be required to play during your games in order to compete successfully against your opponents.

From your very first ends of bowls you will see that the configuration of the 'head' (the layout of the bowls around the jack and the target area for the majority of your bowls played) can vary a great deal. In order for you to play into these varied 'heads' you will need to master a number of basic shots.

## The Draw Shot

This is the most important shot in the game of bowls. It is the shot you must learn to master as a matter of priority. It must become second nature to you. It is your 'bread and butter' shot. Games are very largely won by the players who can draw closer than their opponents. It is a shot that you will most often have to execute, whatever position you are playing. The more confidence you can place in your drawing bowls the more games you will win.

The draw shot can be played on both your forehand and your backhand. To be successful it must be played along the correct line with the correct weight. The target of the draw shot is very often the jack. However, it is also used to achieve other objectives:

- placing a positional bowl in the area of the rink where you think the jack might eventually finish up;
- using a blocking bowl to prevent your opponent getting a clear run at a favourable head.

*Amy Monkhouse, four times winner of the EWBA Champion of Champions, Bronze Medallist at the 2002 and 2006 Commonwealth Games, and 2007 National Indoor Pairs winner, is one of England's brightest rising stars.*
*(Courtesy of Bowls International)*

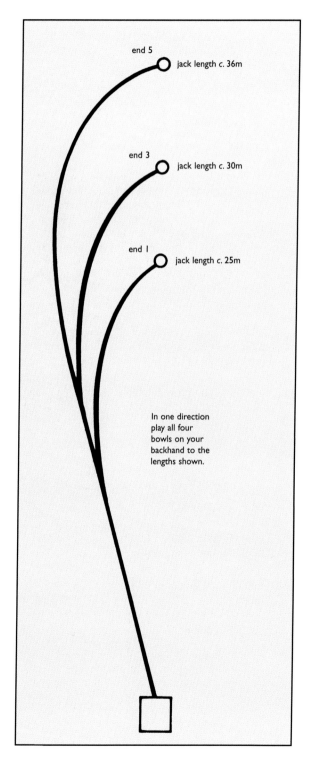

end 5
jack length *c.* 36m

end 3
jack length *c.* 30m

end 1
jack length *c.* 25m

In one direction play all four bowls on your backhand to the lengths shown.

*Fig 8  Drawing to varying lengths.*

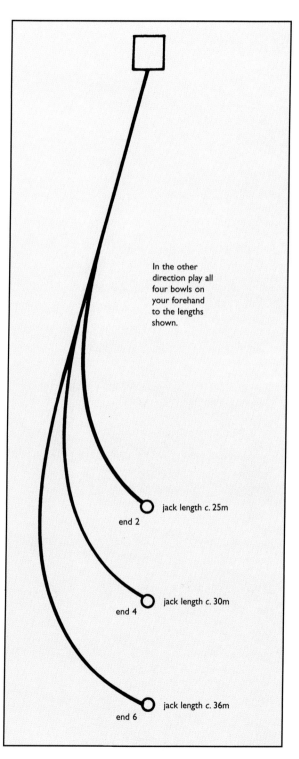

In the other direction play all four bowls on your forehand to the lengths shown.

jack length *c.* 25m
end 2

jack length *c.* 30m
end 4

jack length *c.* 36m
end 6

*Fig 9  Drawing to varying lengths.*

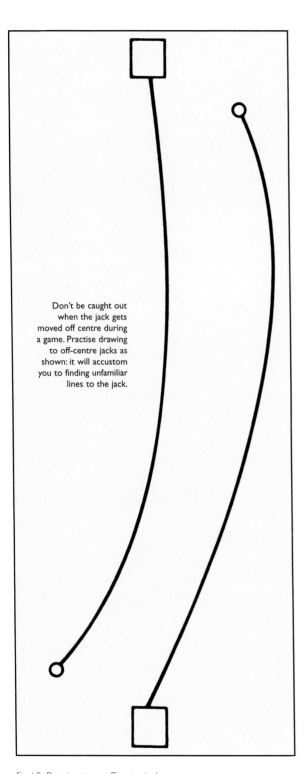

Don't be caught out when the jack gets moved off centre during a game. Practise drawing to off-centre jacks as shown: it will accustom you to finding unfamiliar lines to the jack.

Fig 10 Drawing to an off-centre jack.

Make sure you adhere to the advice given in Chapter 4 concerning the position of your feet and delivery arm in relation to the line you wish to take. Once you are happy that your technique is correct – and don't be frightened to seek the guidance of a qualified coach to confirm you have got it right – then you must practise and practise until you can achieve a success rate of consistently getting four bowls within a metre of the jack.

It is also important that you try to ensure you are equally successful with both your backhand and forehand delivery. It is not unnatural to have a preference. Quite often the backhand shot finds more favour, but you must try to be equally proficient on both hands. You must not believe you are weaker on one hand or you will find yourself restricting your options and becoming tactically and psychologically disadvantaged.

There are certain practices that are particularly good for improving your drawing skills (see Figs 8–10). Those recommended below will soon expose any weaknesses and equally highlight any strengths in your drawing game. You will then be able to work harder on any aspect of your delivery, together with the lengths and lines that are proving more difficult. Again, at this stage the advice of your club/county coach will be very helpful.

This is very basic practice but very valuable. It will allow you to assess your strengths and weaknesses, while helping you to develop both your forehand and backhand play. It will assist you in gaining confidence by getting experience at all lengths.

You should aim to get all four of your bowls within 1m of the jack. Give yourself a point for each bowl that you get within

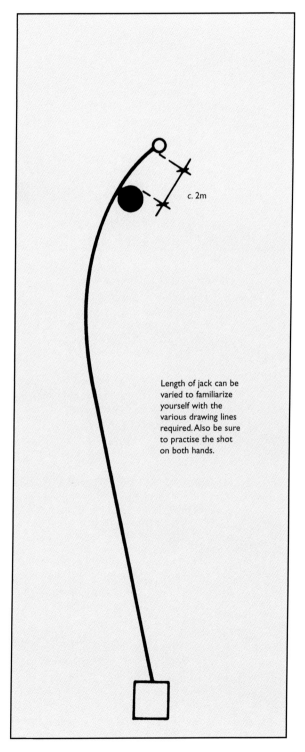

c. 2m

Length of jack can be
varied to familiarize
yourself with the
various drawing lines
required. Also be sure
to practise the shot
on both hands.

*Fig 11   Drawing around a bowl.*

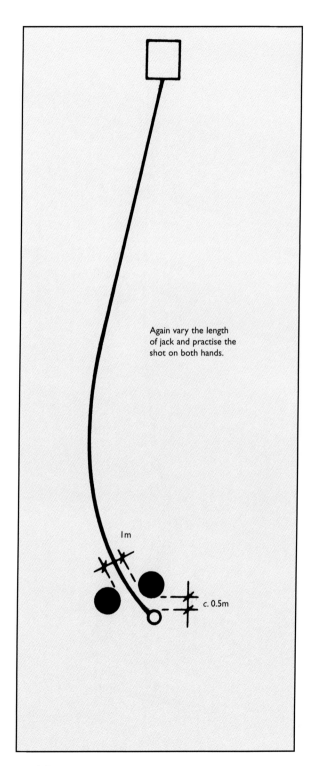

Again vary the length
of jack and practise the
shot on both hands.

1m

c. 0.5m

*Fig 12   Drawing between bowls.*

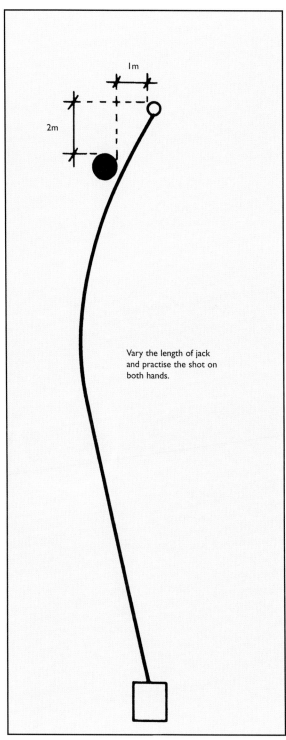

1m

2m

Vary the length of jack
and practise the shot on
both hands.

*Fig 13  Drawing inside a bowl.*

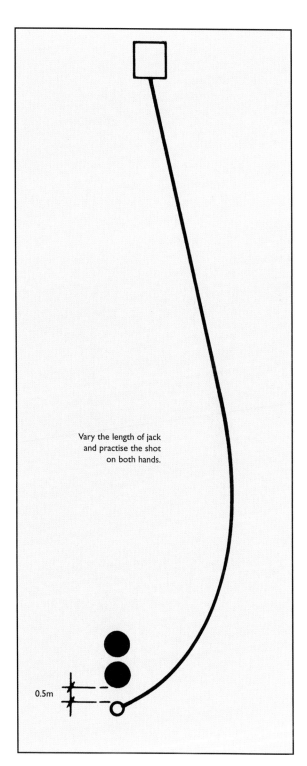

Vary the length of jack
and practise the shot
on both hands.

0.5m

*Fig 14  Drawing to a hidden jack.*

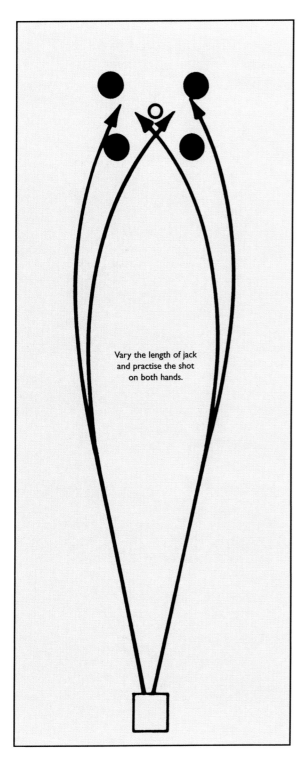

Vary the length of jack
and practise the shot
on both hands.

Fig 15 Drawing within a metre inside or outside bowls.

that distance. If you set yourself a target number of ends to play (say 18), this will give you a total point score to aim for during your practice session. Keep your score and try and improve on that each time you practise. It will add additional interest to your practice session and act as a useful guide to your progress.

Once you have practised a few times drawing to the bare jack you may then find it useful to introduce some positional bowls into the exercise. Placing bowls at certain key points will help to gain experience and confidence in drawing around and inside bowls that are between you and the jack. It is something that you will face in every game you play. Familiarize yourself with these situations in practice and you will be a lot more comfortable with them when you experience them in proper play.

For ways in which you can use strategically placed bowls to assist your drawing skills, see Figs 11–15.

## The Positional Shot

This is a draw shot that is invariably played behind the head to prevent your opponent from capitalizing on his bowls that happen to have finished in one particular area of the rink.

It is an 'insurance' shot to reduce the odds of your opponent picking up shots by trailing the jack through to his waiting back bowls.

Often you will have the choice of hand and a larger target area than normal. If, for example, you only need to produce the best back bowl to reduce the threat of a ditched jack (see Fig 16), you will have a large target area. Do not make the mistake of not selecting a specific target spot. Imagine you are drawing to the jack at whatever spot you select and concentrate on the spot where you want your bowl to finish. If you widen your target area you may not focus well enough and finish too far away from your intended spot (see Fig 17). Be specific, even if you have a little room for error. Lack of focus leads to lack of concentration.

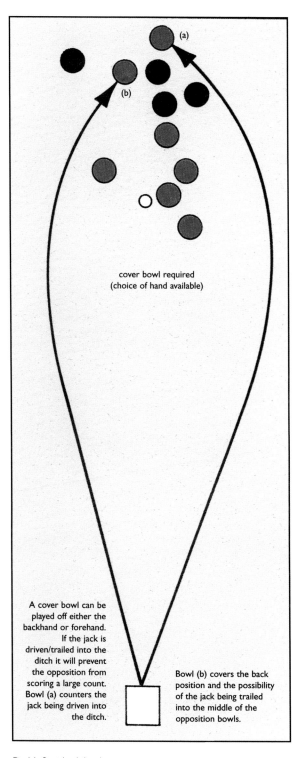

cover bowl required
(choice of hand available)

A cover bowl can be played off either the backhand or forehand. If the jack is driven/trailed into the ditch it will prevent the opposition from scoring a large count. Bowl (a) counters the jack being driven into the ditch.

Bowl (b) covers the back position and the possibility of the jack being trailed into the middle of the opposition bowls.

*Fig 16 Best back bowl.*

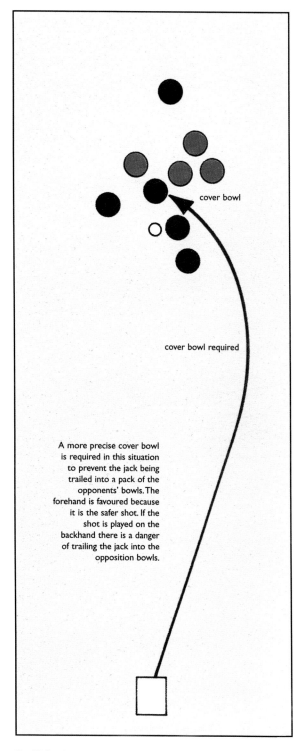

cover bowl

cover bowl required

A more precise cover bowl is required in this situation to prevent the jack being trailed into a pack of the opponents' bowls. The forehand is favoured because it is the safer shot. If the shot is played on the backhand there is a danger of trailing the jack into the opposition bowls.

*Fig 17 Bowl covering a group of opposition bowls.*

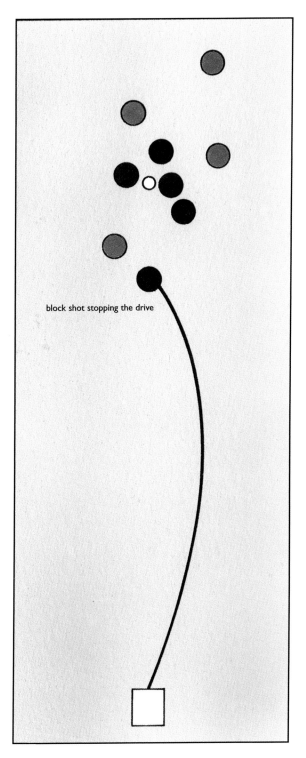

block shot stopping the drive

*Fig 18 The block shot.*

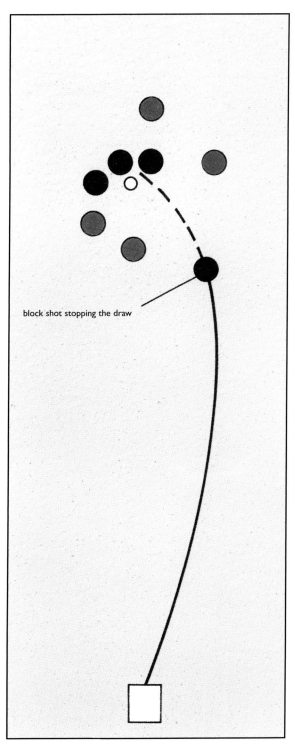

block shot stopping the draw

*Fig 19 The block shot.*

## The Block Shot

Another variation of the draw shot, this is specifically intended to protect your shot bowls, which have been effectively delivered into the head. The block shot should do exactly what it says – block your opponent's line to the target area. This is particularly effective if you have a tight head (bowls very close to the jack), which your opponent is forced to attack with a drive or running bowl. The perfect block shot should be played to a point directly in front of the head and at least 2–3m up the green (see Fig 18). At this distance it reduces the chance of your bowl being driven into the head if it is hit by your opponent's bowl.

Similarly it is often very effective to block the draw (particularly on a good hand). If you are laying shots in a head where there is still a good draw possible to retrieve the shot, it is wise to protect your position. More times than not, if you leave an able player a good open hand to draw shot on he will usually do just that. This particular shot does not necessarily have to be right on the draw line (see Fig 19). Sometimes a bowl 15–30cm off the line will be sufficient to distract your opponent. It can often have a psychological effect resulting in your opponent over-adjusting and straying too far from the required line.

Again you must pick the specific spot where you intend your block shot to finish. Your target must not be a wide area. This will assist you to choose the correct line.

---

### USEFUL TIP

In order to place a block shot on the draw line, you will need to aim wider than your normal draw line to the centre of the rink. Don't forget to point your feet a little wider along your new wider draw line (see Fig 20).

---

## The Trail Shot

This is a shot using very controlled weight. It is most often used to trail the jack within, or just through, the head to your waiting bowls. It is one of the most effective shots for getting a maximum result in terms of converting the head to your advantage. The art of the shot lies in fully controlling the weight of your bowl. It must have sufficient weight to trail the jack – half a metre, 1m, 2–3m – wherever it is going to reap maximum benefit. It must, however, not be played with too much weight, which will destroy the head or remove the jack too far away from your waiting bowls.

Your practice in perfecting your draw shot will stand you in good stead for mastering the trail shot. It is, after all, essentially an extension of the draw and not a weight shot. There are specific exercises to assist you to perfect this very influential shot (see Figs 21 and 22).

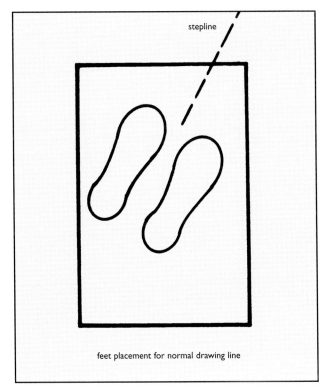

feet placement for normal drawing line

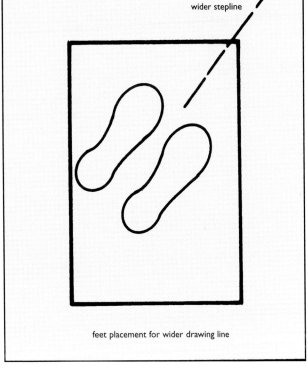

feet placement for wider drawing line

*Fig 20.*

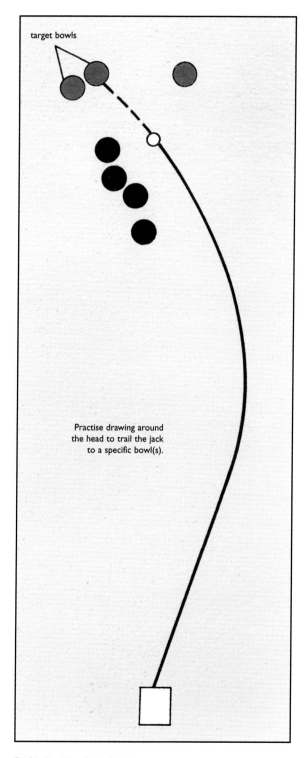

target bowls

Practise drawing around
the head to trail the jack
to a specific bowl(s).

Fig 21  Practising the trail shot.

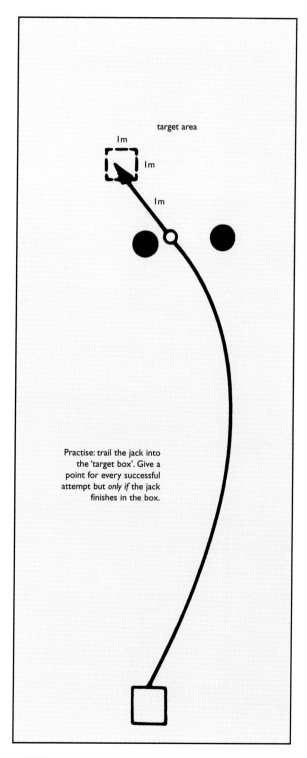

target area

1m

1m

1m

Practise: trail the jack into
the 'target box'. Give a
point for every successful
attempt but only if the jack
finishes in the box.

Fig 22  Practising the trail shot.

# Over the Draw – the 'Yard On' Shot

This is another extension to the draw shot. It is a very versatile shot that is used to strengthen and alter heads in a positive manner in a number of different ways. It is a shot that has proved invaluable in the outdoor game. On heavier greens it proves a very positive shot that ensures players reach up to and through the head. It is, however, what it says it is – a 'yard on' shot. It is frequently

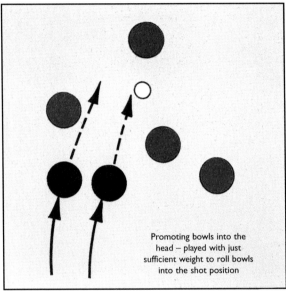

Promoting bowls into the head – played with just sufficient weight to roll bowls into the shot position

Fig 23.

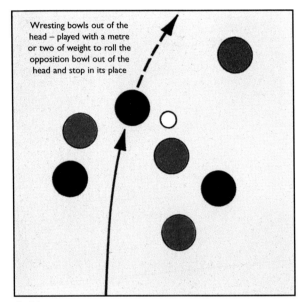

Wresting bowls out of the head – played with a metre or two of weight to roll the opposition bowl out of the head and stop in its place

Fig 24.

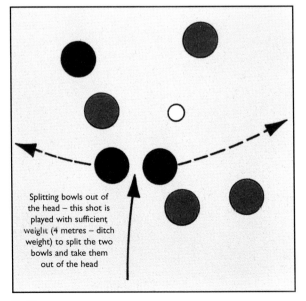

Splitting bowls out of the head – this shot is played with sufficient weight (4 metres – ditch weight) to split the two bowls and take them out of the head

Fig 25.

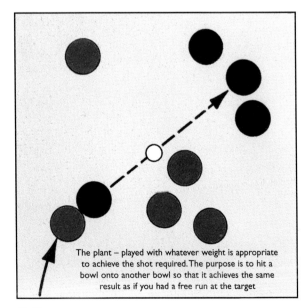

The plant – played with whatever weight is appropriate to achieve the shot required. The purpose is to hit a bowl onto another bowl so that it achieves the same result as if you had a free run at the target

Fig 26.

requested by the skip of a rink and this is all too frequently interpreted as a request for a fully fledged controlled weight shot that can be anything up to ditch length. It must again be played with very controlled weight or, like the trail shot, it will not achieve its purpose. Played correctly it can be used to:

- Promote bowls into the head (see Fig 23);
- Wrest bowls out of the head (see Fig 24);
- Split bowls out of the head (see Fig 25);
- Plant bowls into the head (see Fig 26).

It has many benefits in building a favourable head. If it reaches the head with no contact with any bowls it ensures you have a well-placed positional bowl just behind the head. If contact is made the weight is such that it will still have the right momentum to reach and stay in the head. Bowls in the head are vital at all times and are directly proportionate to your chances of winning.

## The 'Heavy' Weight Shots

On most occasions these shots are used to get you out of trouble when the shot(s) and head are against you. However, you may also opt to use one to take an opposition shot bowl out when it is preventing you from scoring a few shots. A firm bowl with ditch weight or more, requiring a narrower and more direct line to the target, may be considered to be the easier shot with the best chance of success. This will be particularly the case if the drawing hands are not bending consistently and it would be difficult to gauge the line for a 'yard on' or 'two yard on' shot.

Equally, if you have a lot of back bowls you may wish to hit the jack into the ditch, giving you a significant count. A full-blooded drive or a controlled shot with ditch weight (allowing the bowl to bend a little) will both give you the result you require. Which one you select is usually down to individual preference (whichever shot you feel more confident in playing), tempered with the knowledge of how the rink is reacting to running bowls.

*Step distances vary according to whether you are playing a draw (above) or a drive (right).*
(© Paul Walker)

## The Drive

The mighty 'drive' is both feared and despised by the purists of the game. It is, however, a very important and necessary shot to have in your bowling armoury. To execute it effectively you must deliver your bowl with sufficient force to counteract the bias so that it travels as directly as possible to the target object. It is normally used to destroy a particularly unfavourable head. It is your spectacular 'get out of jail' card if the opposition have outplayed you and have left you with no option but to play with extreme weight. Its forceful nature is its strength. It needs to inflict as much damage to the head as possible. If it misses its specific target in the head, its brute force will more than likely ensure it still gets a beneficial result by hitting adjacent bowls. Its substantial momentum will carry it through the head, disturbing as many bowls as possible. Some might say it is not a pretty sight to behold, but it is a very welcome one if it gets you out of trouble. Skips rightly use the shot a lot and must be adept at it. At first sight it appears to be an easy shot to play in which the usual mental calculation relating bend to distance seems straightforward – no bend and as quick as you can bowl it. It is not.

You must adapt your delivery technique to enable you to achieve consistently good drives. The key to success is making sure your foot placement is correct (see Fig 27). The driving arm follows where the front foot goes and a pronounced follow through of that arm is important in perfecting the drive. It naturally follows that if you step down the wrong line the fast arm movement will follow and you will miss. Step narrow and you will miss on the narrow side. You must try to step forward in line with your target object so your driving arm can whip through past your foot on a line that will take your bowl directly to the target.

The line you take, and which you step down, will be directly related to the speed with which you drive. If you do not drive fast you will need to step down a line that allows your bowl an appropriate small degree of bend.

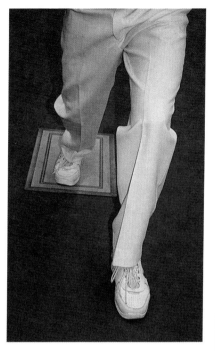

*Slightly wider step for a slower, less direct drive.*
*(© Paul Walker)*

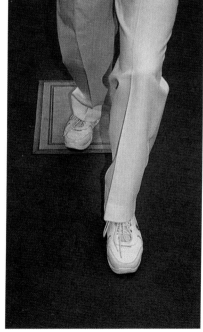

*Step for a direct drive.*
*(© Paul Walker)*

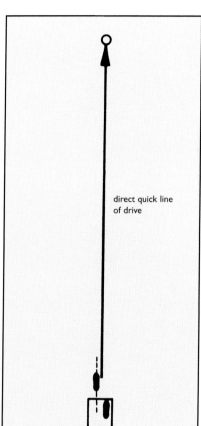

direct quick line
of drive

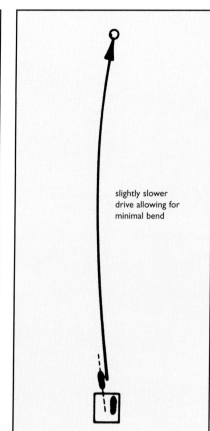

slightly slower
drive allowing for
minimal bend

*Fig 27  Drive lines.*

## How Fast Should You Drive?

There is no speed limit on bowling greens. Nevertheless every bowler should be aware of their driving limitations, since if you try to drive too fast you will lose control of the bowl and it will miss its line. It is important to remember that in playing this shot bowlers impart a considerable amount of body weight in a forward direction at the moment they release the bowl. This extra weight must be carefully controlled so that there is no loss of balance, allowing the bowling arm to come through in an exact line and with the exact speed. Stepping a little further forward will gain you some force, but it is important that you do not increase the length of your forward stride too much, as this will also result in a loss of balance. So while the drive is the most animated shot you will have to play, your delivery movements must still be disciplined and controlled.

You must practise the driving shot and work out which is the optimum speed for you to use. Start off with as quick a delivery as you can and then slow your deliveries little by little to establish your optimum driving speed, namely the speed at which you have the highest strike rate.

Another useful self-analysis tool is to insert a distinct pause between the arm and foot movement (see Fig 28). This allows you to focus on the line to the target and the foot placement in the first instance. The arm movement is then brought into play at varying speeds. You can then start to eliminate the pause until, by trial and error, you have developed a well coordinated movement at a speed that suits your delivery action.

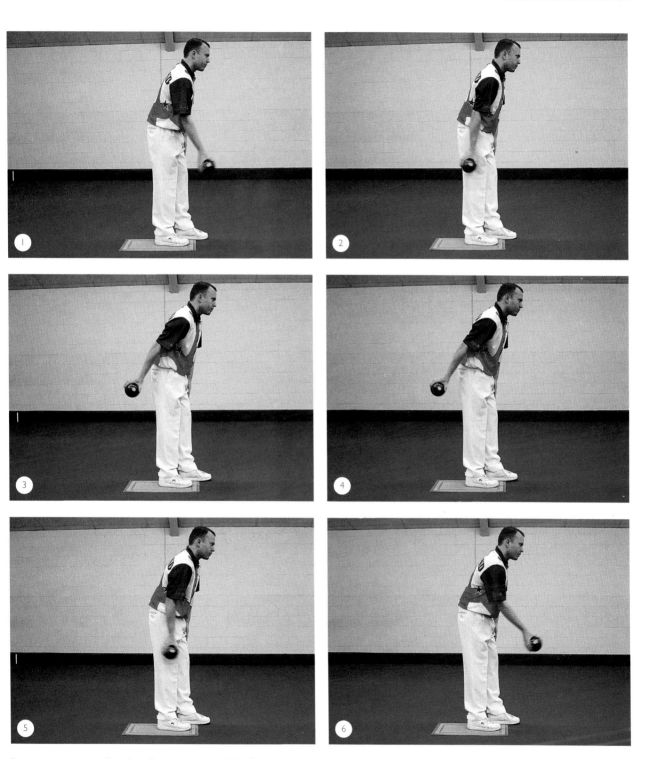

*Best practice sequence for a drive. Correct positioning of the feet is essential in order to drive successfully (photographs 1–16).*
(© Paul Walker)

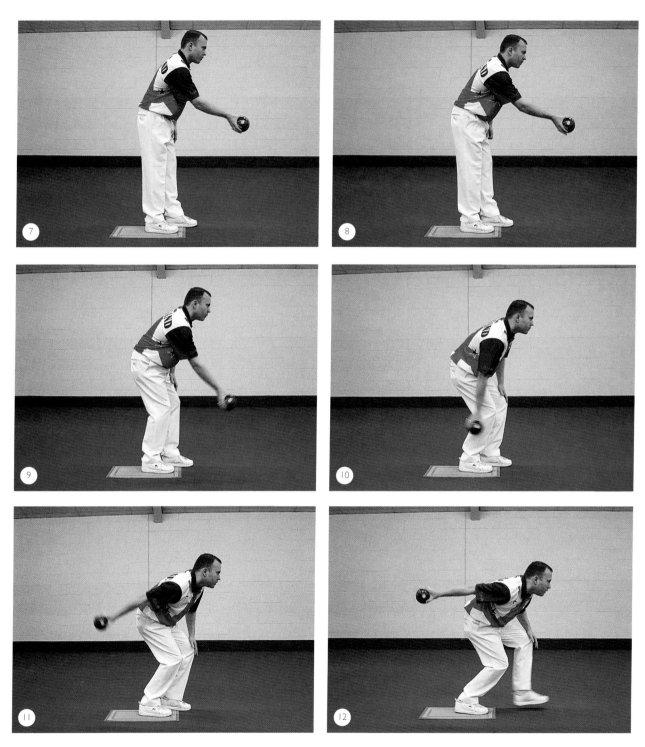

Best practice sequence for a drive. Correct positioning of the feet is essential in order to drive successfully (photographs 1–16 continued).
(© Paul Walker)

### USEFUL TIP

The outcome of the drive, because of its very nature, can be very unpredictable. Always expect the unexpected, and however safe you may think your only bowl in the head is – it never is. Use the shot sensibly, not as a matter of course. It is almost a last resort.

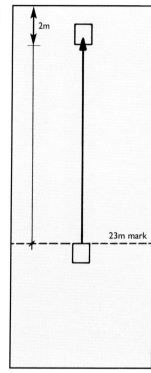

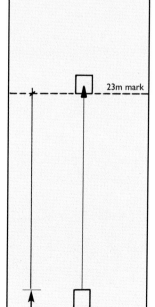

Your target can be a mat, or two bowls placed 300mm apart with the jack in between. Using a mat is easier as the bowls and jack have to be set up again each time they are hit.

**Purposeful Practice**

Driving practice at the lengths shown – drive with four bowls on the backhand, then forehand and then alternate hands with each bowl.

Your objective is to hit the target mat with all four balls.

Check your success rate, and ascertain which is your best driving hand.

*Fig 28  Purposeful practice for driving.*

## The 'Firm' or 'Controlled Weight' Shot

This controlled weight shot can be played with a variety of weights. It is quite often appropriate to choose the weight that you think will give you the best line in to your objective. It is usually more important to hit the target rather than to worry about the precise weight to be used. It can be used effectively to remove opponents' bowls from the head. It is also commonly used to open up unfavourable heads and to retrieve heads where you wish to change the shape of the head rather than destroy it.

As with the drive shot, a slightly longer step forward will increase your back swing and help you deliver the bowl with the extra weight you require. Again a pronounced follow through with the bowling arm along the delivery line will benefit the successful execution of the shot.

---

**USEFUL TIP**

Don't become too dependent on the weighted shot. Overuse of the heavy shots will have an adverse effect on your drawing capabilities. It is difficult to revert to a drawing rhythm after a series of drives or weight shots.

---

## Shot Selection and Building a Good Head

You should now be aware of the shots you will be called upon to play during your games. How you select which shot to play will depend entirely on the circumstances prevailing at the time you play that shot. You must always be attentive and perceptive. You must not only assess the position of the bowls and jack at the head as they are, you must plan ahead by anticipating your opponents' next shot(s) and assessing what the outcome may be. You can then look at your options and decide whether you play into the head or play a covering/blocking bowl that will counter your opponent's next bowl(s). You will of course be advised and 'directed' by your skip in team games, but you must learn to judge the head and tactics for yourself. Good shot selection, building the head and tactical play improve with experience and there is no substitute for 'being there', 'doing that' and seeing the consequences unravel at first hand. Nevertheless, I will try and provide you with a set of guidelines that will assist in promoting good practice in your tactical deliberations. These, when read alongside the roles of individual positions in Chapter 7, will constitute a set of general principles that will help you to play the game properly and, it is to be hoped, successfully.

Never forget bowls is basically a simple game. In all games you are trying to outbowl your opposition. To win you must finish up with more bowls nearer the jack than your opponent(s). However, remember there are a lot of ends to achieve that. Be patient and don't get paranoid about winning every end, or losing a shot. Remember the fable of 'the tortoise and the hare', since in bowls the tortoise often sticks its head out of its shell at the finishing line! So when you are one shot down, with a difficult position to face, be content to lose a shot. It could be worse if you try to retrieve shot and give more shots away or leave the position exposed for your opponent to capitalize on. (This scenario assumes, of course, that it is not the last end and you are all square or losing.)

From the very first bowl of any game – single, pairs, triples or fours – you are trying to build a head of bowls that will succeed both in preventing the opposition from scoring and in producing as many shots as possible for yourself or your team (see Figs 29 and 30). The better the head, the more shots you are likely to score. The worse it is the more you are likely to lose – this is obvious but very true. Remember, too, games are often won by the number of shots you lose. By keeping the shots you lose to a minimum you will invariably triumph. Losing single shots is anything but disastrous and can be easily recovered. Losing significant counts is different and normally very costly. It invariably puts games beyond redemption. Learning to build and protect good heads, and to select the most effective shots to do that, will maximize your chances of winning games.

There are a number of key factors that influence the construction of a good head:

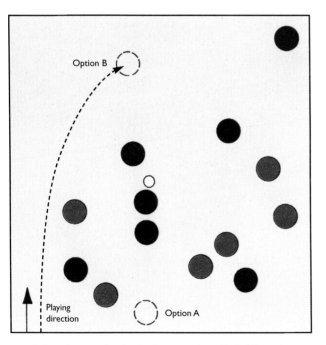

A classic favourable 'head' – the drawing hands are blocked. The jack is protected. the back position is covered, along with the area immediately behind the jack. It is only a one bowl target if weight is being considered. If there are two bowls to come and you are holding shot and it is your turn to play you have the happy choice of protecting the position with a blocker (Option A) or adding another back bowl (Option B).

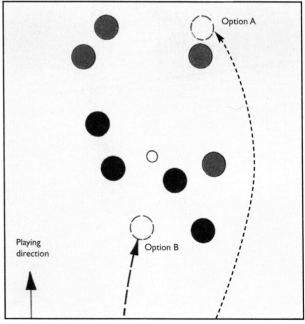

Although holding 2 shots the position is highly vulnerable to a running shot on the backhand which would take the jack through to three waiting opposition bowls. Action required – a cover bowl (first priority) at the back to split the opposition bowls (Option A) and if you have another bowl, protect the head by blocking the line in (Option B).

*Fig 29  A good head.*

*Fig 30  A vulnerable head.*

- You need good bowls in the head early. If you produce bowls that are touching or near to the jack at the very start of the end, you will usually dictate how that end will be played. You are in control until the position is altered, by which time you will have had the opportunity to cover the positions where the jack may finish up. Dictating the head also puts immediate pressure on the opposition. It is a proven fact that from a psychological point of view it is a lot easier to draw a shot when you are already lying shot than it is when shot is against. This is particularly true in the case of the skip, who can become agitated and unsettled if he finds himself continually going to the mat with shot(s) against. Learn the lesson – concentrate really hard on getting to the jack first.
- Another golden rule is very obvious. Do not play short bowls. They have almost no chance of scoring, and inevitably finish up blocking your own line in to the jack. In certain heavy conditions it is understandable for your first bowl to be short, but you should always ensure you make the necessary adjustment with your second. If you err with weight you must do so on the 'long side'. Bowls through the head can always be useful. Short bowls are one of the biggest contributing factors to losing games.
- Always choose the easiest line to the jack. Play the open hand unless there are special circumstances when you need to do otherwise. The open hand will involve the simple and straightforward mental assessment of how to get your bowl to the target. Playing around or inside bowls complicates this process. The easiest shot is nearly always the right one.
- Assess which hands on the rink are the easiest to play and utilize them as much as possible. Again, keep life simple and play the easiest hands.
- Don't be afraid to be positive. Attack the head if shots are against. You must,

of course, temper this decision with a proper assessment of the position. However, if you are not over-vulnerable, for example if there is only one bowl in the head or there are no back bowls, then playing positively will pay far more dividends than being too cautious. 'Nothing ventured, nothing gained' is very much applicable. Make sure you fully weigh up all implications of a positive shot, but don't be too negative. A 'brave heart' has won far more than a faint one (much of the success of the Scotland teams at all levels can be attributed to such an approach).

- Consolidate your early position in the head. Never leave yourself exposed by having only one bowl in the head. Not only will it give the opposition the chance to capitalize on the situation and remove it for a count, it will inhibit your own choice of shot. It will invariably limit you to a draw as you cannot risk taking your own bowl out with a heavy shot.
- Always be on the look out for 'danger areas', those parts of the rink where you are particularly vulnerable. It may be where a number of opposition bowls have finished together or perhaps the rear of the rink, where opposition bowls may be scattered across it without any of your own being present. The important thing is for you to ensure that you always cover these areas with a 'positional' bowl to reduce your vulnerability.
- Use your strengths. Some of the particular shots that you and your teammates have developed and perfected will be better than others. In choosing the shot to play make sure your judgement takes this into account when, for example, you might be called on to play a weight shot to open up the head. If you are comfortable playing with a 'yard on' but particularly good at playing the 'ditch weight' shot, then play to your strength. Your chances of success are directly related to the confidence you have in playing the

shots. All things being equal, that confidence will always be boosted by playing the shots you know you can play well.

---

**KEY POINT**

Make sure your draw shot is one of your strengths. It is of primary importance in every game and position you play.

---

# Summary

Your choice of shot and tactical assessment will first and foremost be determined by the disposition of the bowls on the rink, along with the options available to consolidate, protect or retrieve the shot. These will change each end. Your judgement of the situation and subsequent action to be taken need to reflect many factors. It is to be hoped the guidelines above will provide you with a basic understanding of these and guide you in using your bowls effectively, along with a very basic framework for building a favourable head. These are the building blocks for success. You must ensure you become fully engrossed in the 'mechanics' of the game. Building a good head and 'reading' the game well (employing the best tactics) undoubtedly wins games. They are fully interrelated and inseparable. You must follow how the heads develop and how the end unfolds. Important though it is, you will see there is more to the game than just drawing close to the jack. This will become increasingly apparent the more you play the game and as you come to appreciate another inevitable fact: you can never predict precisely what is going to happen to a head when it is hit by a heavy bowl. Nevertheless, if you follow the guidelines outlined above you are well on the way to preparing for most contingencies and developing a proper understanding of the game.

PART 3
# PLAYING THE GAME

# CHAPTER 6

# THE FOUR PLAYING DISCIPLINES

You now have a basic grasp of the general principles involved in applying the shots you have learnt to play. You are ready to play the game in earnest.

There are four types of game you can be involved in: singles, pairs, triples and fours. They are all different and involve varying positional skills and tactics. We shall deal with these in Chapter 7, where the positional roles in particular will be explained in detail so that you know what is expected of you if you choose (or are chosen) to play in any particular one.

## Proper Preparation

Whatever game you are involved in, you must ensure you prepare yourself properly. This might be as simple as making sure you arrive in plenty of time before the game. Many games are lost because the player has been delayed, or mistimed the journey time, and he has to rush into the club and right onto the green. This naturally does not allow any time to compose yourself or mentally prepare yourself for the game. As a result

you may get off to a bad start from which you never recover.

Many players have set routines that they go through meticulously before a game. Some will always polish their bowls and walk to a quiet area of the club or green for a period of personal contemplation. Others will find an area where they can undertake some warming-up exercises. Some like to sit and watch the game in progress on the rink on which they are about to play. When I had the luxury of adequate time before a

England's Stephen Farish and Australia's Kelvin Kerkow being congratulated by the author after their 2006 Commonwealth Games Semi-Final in Melbourne. Kelvin Kerkow went on to win the Gold Medal.
(© John Bell)

singles game I used to ensure I had a hot relaxing bath before leaving home. I would then play my favourite songs in the car on the way to the game.

You must do what you consider works best for you. Whatever that may be, it must ensure that you are as relaxed, yet focused, as possible. Stressful situations must be avoided at all costs. There must be no last-minute disruptions: no arguments about playing positions, no forgotten items of equipment, no panic over which bowls to play with, and certainly no missing team members. Careful and simple preparation will ensure these are avoided and greatly assist your chances of success.

## Singles

Players: 2
Bowls: 4 each
Format: First player to score 21 shots wins, playing as many ends as necessary
Variations:
(1) 2 bowls singles games are also played.
(2) The television tournaments and the qualifiers for these, as well as other select competitions, play the 'Sets' game. This normally involves playing two nine-end 'sets'. The winner is the player who wins both sets (or one set and a draw). Should the score be one set all, then a series of three tiebreak ends are played. Whoever wins the end scores a point.

The player with most points wins. It is a game that was specially manufactured for television. Its duration is controlled and it has more climaxes (end of set and tiebreak dramas) to excite the media and spectators, and it serves this purpose well. It was used extensively in the media-orientated 2006 Commonwealth Games in Melbourne.

This variation of the singles game, however, has not won the general support of grassroots bowls or indeed many of the top bowlers who participate in televised events. It is seen as a game that leaves too much to chance and one that often does not reflect the run of play. As with many

The impressive 'portable rink' used for the WBT televised tournaments.
(Courtesy of Bowls International)

arguments, there are pros and cons. The fact remains that from a television point of view 'sets' play is here to stay for the reasons stated. Its application elsewhere is basically down to who wants to adopt it. Our club, for instance, plays the best of

three 'nine shots up' sets in our Two Wood competition. It works well and is popular. Our club championship is the traditional 21 shots up. The 'sets' format therefore is a variation that can refresh traditional practices if required.

## Playing Singles

The singles game is a bowling education in itself. It will improve your overall play and prove to be a great character builder as well. It can seem a long and lonely experience, but it is a game that will develop your overall potential like no other. Make no mistake, it is exacting. You will need to use all the shots from your 'bowling arsenal' and it will ask searching questions of your bowling temperament. If you respond in a totally positive and measured manner, however, you will enhance both your bowling skills and confidence.

## Psychological Strengths

No other game in our sport requires as much self-control as the singles game. You are out there on your own. All the decisions are yours. There is no one else on the green to motivate and encourage you. You must be mentally strong and psychologically well prepared. Given the importance of this mental state, it is worth spelling out the key psychological qualities I have observed in the best singles players in the world. To be really successful at singles play you must learn to develop the following mental attributes.

### Lasting Concentration

Your concentration must not waver throughout the duration of the game. You are twenty all in a big match. You have a bare yard to draw the winner with your last bowl. Even worse, you are also one shot down and game lie against. You need to draw the shot. You need the ability to focus even harder on the task in hand and save the game. Your concentration needs to be as sharp as when you started.

### Mental Toughness

It is this that enables you to cope with difficult incidents. You are laying four good shots and your opponent's bowl is a yard off line. He gets an edge from an outside bowl, picks up the jack and he gets four shots instead. You need to be tough enough

*David Bryant CBE. The ultimate singles specialist and absolute master of concentration. His singles wins include: three World Outdoor titles, three World Indoor titles, four Commonwealth Games titles, 15 English titles (nine indoor and six outdoor) and eight British Isles titles (four indoor and four outdoor); a remarkable list of achievements from a phenomenal bowler.*
*(Courtesy of Bowls International)*

to dismiss it from your mind and get on with the game as though nothing had happened. The ability to remain composed in spite of everything is a marvellous asset. It might not be something that comes easily, but come it must.

## Ability to Be Patient

There is no need to start worrying if your opponent is winning ends with single shots. There is no finite number of ends prescribed to achieve your 21 shots. Be patient and keep grinding away. If you are playing good bowls, but not getting the shot, your time will come – your opportunities will arise. Do not become frustrated. This will affect your composure and concentration.

## Totally Realistic Approach

Concentrate on the things that you can influence. You cannot control the uncontrollable; the weather, the green or an outrageous fluke, for example, are all out of your control. You have to accept the conditions and outcomes you get and make the best of them. It is no good putting yourself under more pressure, or upsetting yourself and your concentration by feeling aggrieved about such factors. Dismiss these from your mind and be positive.

## Positive State of Mind

You must remain positive at all times, parti-cularly if you fall behind during the game. As explained above, comebacks are always possible, but only if you remain positive and never succumb until the final shot is scored against you. Don't dwell on your bad bowls either. Let them go out of your mind and concentrate on your next ones.

## Lack of Complacency

Never underestimate your opponent. Complacency undermines performance. It leads to lack of concentration and focus and it will have an adverse effect on your game. Equally never underestimate your opponent's ability to play a particular shot. 'He'll never get that', those famous last words, is often heard as you are putting a number of opposition shots on the card. If you do not cover a vulnerable position, you gamble at your own risk.

*Mark Walton is a prolific English National Championship winner, including two singles titles, and World Outdoor Champion of Champions winner.*
(Courtesy of Bowls International)

### Self-Belief

Before you beat your opponent you must be able to beat yourself. Any negative thought on your part is a positive contribution to the potential success of your opponent. You will never succeed properly if you do not believe in yourself and your ability to play the shots. This belief directly affects your performance. Self-belief breeds confidence. Confidence produces shots on the card.

### Will to win

The great golfer Arnold Palmer said 'winning isn't everything, but wanting to is'. It directly affects your concentration in a positive way. It can make the difference in how well you play a shot. If you really want to get the shot, the extra effort in concentration and determination you put in will really pay dividends. It will enable you to play that crucial shot at the critical moment when it is required.

### Composure

According to David Bryant, 'Bowls is about controlled aggression'. The will to win will keep the adrenaline flowing, particularly when you are required to play an especially important bowl. It is then, however, that you need to exert some self-control. The art of composing yourself at these moments is vital. You need to be totally relaxed on the mat so that you can play your shot unfettered by the mental and physical tension of the situation. How can you put the pressures and distractions of the 'big moment' to one side? It is something you must ultimately work out for yourself. Different players address the situation in different ways. Experience is a large part of the answer. Being in 'that situation' before always helps. You always learn from pain – and painful some of these experiences can be. You're winning 20–17 and you lose four shots when you had 2 yards to draw the shot. That's something you don't forget. It leaves a mental scar. I guarantee the next time you face a similar situation you will be better prepared, since you have endured that experience before. The more times you face tense situations the better you should become at addressing them. As a general rule, many players find that taking a few deep breaths before you play your bowl helps to ease the tension and assists concentration. Find what works for you, but always think positive. If you think you will fail, more often than not you will.

## Playing Guidelines for Singles

You are aware of the demanding psychological requirements, all of which also apply to the other disciplines (but not to the same intensity). Once you have ensured you are in the right positive frame of mind you are ready to digest the playing principles involved in the singles game.

First and foremost, you must be very clear about which particular personal playing strengths you are going to use to give you the most effective competitive edge for your singles games. Which lengths do you play best? Which hand are you most comfortable with when playing your drawing shots? What is your most effective

*An indoor specialist, Carol Ashby is a great competitor establishing herself in the ladies' competitive scene. She has won two WBT Ladies Singles and four English National Indoor Singles titles.*
(Courtesy of Bowls International)

weight shot and do you play it better on the backhand or forehand? Which bowls are best suited to the playing surface involved? Have you any detailed knowledge about the way that surface plays? Such vital information is needed to formulate your initial game plan. The strengths and weaknesses of your opponent must also be quickly ascertained over the first few ends of the game. Your game plan must adequately reflect this as well, and as such must be flexible in nature. You must always be alert and able to respond to the circumstances and outcomes arising during your games. With these underlying principles in mind, the following guidelines will provide you with the essential building blocks to enable you to work on your game, and to develop the necessary skills and techniques to become a competent and successful singles player.

- Singles is essentially a drawing game. You need to be particularly proficient with the draw shot – at all lengths. You need to be able to play both backhand and forehand effortlessly. You must be able to vary the mat and jack position in order to extend or shorten the jack length to suit your strengths and your opponent's weaknesses. You must be able to deliver the jack to the length you require.
- The more consistently you draw then the better the heads you will build, and the less need there will be for difficult conversion and retrieval shots. The more you draw well the easier it is to sustain a drawing rhythm and focused frame of mind. Don't become preoccupied with weight shots until your draw is under control.
- Your first bowl is the most important bowl. If you can draw a toucher or close bowl with it you put pressure on your opponent from the very start of the end. If you repeat the exercise with your second you dictate the way the end will now be played out. Take time at the start of every end to compose yourself and give maximum concentration to your first bowl.
- Do not play short bowls.
- Should you fail to beat your opponent to the jack and he is dictating play, then your objective is to draw as close as you can to the jack and shot bowl. A good second shot in these circumstances is very acceptable. Losing single shots is not a disaster by any means. Losing your head and running at your opponent's shot bowl and missing with all your bowls is. Play safe and avoid losing big scores at all costs.
- You must be consistent in your play. Try to settle on a good length by quickly adjusting to the pace of the green. Play up and down one side of the rink if the hands are good. The pace will be the same and aid your consistency. Consistent length play will generally enable you to avoid losing those big counts, but don't forget to cover the back position if you are vulnerable there.
- As a general rule, do not try to follow the line of your opponent. His delivery and/or his bowls might be completely different to yours. Find your own line. If you are playing on your opponent's green, however, it may be prudent to play the same side of the green as him (he will know the best hands), but still find your own line.
- Assess the playing qualities and characteristics of the rink as quickly as

*John Price, the Welsh 'Mr Consistency', has been the World Indoor Singles winner, ten times winner of the Welsh Indoor Singles title and a World Indoor Pairs winner with Stephen Rees.*
*(Courtesy of Bowls International)*

possible. If all goes well you may be able to do this during the trial ends. You may find it useful to arrive at the green a little earlier and observe the rink you are about to play on. If not, use the first three or four ends of the game to identify the best hands that suit your bowls and delivery style. Stick with these hands as much as possible.

- Don't waste bowls by playing the shots that are markedly not suited to the conditions – the faster the green the less you should play controlled weight shots. Don't be too cautious on slow greens; make sure you are up to the head.

- There is a strong possibility that at some time you will need to play heavy bowls to get yourself out of trouble. Make sure you have practised these shots and have full confidence in them. As always, play to your strengths. If you are particularly good at driving then use it when a heavy shot is required – don't be tempted to play anything less. (This obviously does not apply when an overweight trail shot is required.)

- If the head is building up against you, use your third bowl to open it up. This always leaves your fourth bowl to retrieve or minimize any collateral damage.

- Take your time and play the game at your own pace. Don't be rushed into playing too fast. Slowing the game down (without contravening the rules) can often help to disrupt your opponent's rhythm, particularly if he is on a scoring spree.

- Be prepared to alter the pattern of the game. If you are finding it difficult to score, change the length, play more aggressively or change the mat position. Even if you are playing well on a length, but are not scoring, change the 'shape' of the game.

- Make sure you utilize the 'percentage' shot to the full. This is the shot that will give you a good result even if it does not achieve the exact objective you intended. Do not waste opportunities by trying to be too precise and neglecting to play the 'percentage' bowl.

*Three times Outdoor World Singles Champion and three times World Pairs Champion, Ireland's Margaret Johnston* MBE *is the most accomplished lady bowler in the world; and one of the better exponents of the weight shot in the ladies' game.*
*(Courtesy of Bowls International)*

---

**USEFUL TIP**

Play with someone of at least equal playing stature, or ideally someone better, in order to improve.

- As a general rule, if you win the end then give the jack away and opt to have the last bowl. This does not apply if your opponent is throwing the jack to a length that you are struggling to find, in which case you must take the jack and change the length. You will find, however, that it is generally a tremendous advantage to have the last bowl, particularly if you are playing well.
- Always make sure you are well informed about the position at the head. If you are not sure about anything, go up and look for yourself.
- Lastly, condition yourself to enjoy, and thrive on, singles games in front of spectators. If you are successful as a singles player (or player in general) you will play in games that attract crowds. Make sure you use the occasion in the spotlight to lift your game and not detract from it. There is no better feeling than playing well in front of many spectators. Learn to feed on the experience. Go out to impress and savour the moment. Be inspired, not overawed.

While it is to be hoped these guidelines will assist you, there is no substitute for getting out there and experiencing these situations, and putting the theory into practice.

Steve Glasson, a World Outdoor Singles winner and a prolific Australian title winner, is one of the most accomplished southern hemisphere singles players.
(© John Bell)

> **USEFUL TIP**
>
> For purposeful practice to improve your singles play, work on the exercises identified for leads, seconds and skips (see Chapter 7).

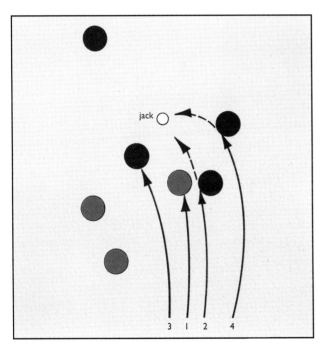

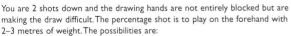

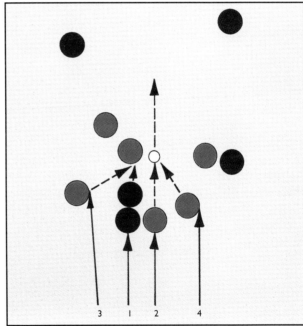

You are 2 shots down and the drawing hands are not entirely blocked but are making the draw difficult. The percentage shot is to play on the forehand with 2–3 metres of weight. The possibilities are:
1. Promotion of your own bowl up for shot
2. Split and follow through, pushing your own bowl onto the shot bowl and easing it out of the head. Your own bowl could also follow through for shot
3. Chop and lie onto the shot bowl
4. If you are wide you might get a good connection on the second shot bowl.

*Fig 31 Percentage weight shot.*

You are at least 3 shots down but it is a packed head and a drive will give you a number of possible results, all favourable:
1. Direct plant onto the shot bowl and possibly the jack as well
2. Opposition bowl onto jack and into ditch
3. If slightly tight you might get a ride back off the bowl onto the shot and/or jack
4. If wide you might drive the short bowl across onto the jack. You might also follow through off it, if you hit it at the right angle.

*Fig 32 Percentage drive shot.*

## Pairs, Triples and Fours

By the very nature of the different number of players and bowls involved, the other three playing disciplines (pairs, triples and fours) all have their individual characteristics. The principles regarding tactics and positional play, however, are very similar. (For an insight into the way these disciplines should be played, see the section on Shot Selection and Building a Good Head in Chapter 5, along with the comprehensive analysis of Positional Play in Chapter 7.)

### Pairs

Players each side:  2 (lead and skip)
Bowls per player:  4
Format:  21 ends duration
Variations:
(1)  Number of ends can vary according to the local situation, e.g. reduced for local leagues/tournaments.
(2)  Two bowl pairs in the 'sets' format are played in the TV tournaments and were played at the 2006 Commonwealth Games.

### Triples

Players each side:  3 (lead, second and skip)
Bowls per player:  3
Format:  18 ends duration
Variations:
(1)  2 bowl triples are sometimes played in domestic competitions.
(2)  Ends may vary according to local situation.

### Fours

Players each side:  4 (lead, second, third and skip)
Bowls per player:  2
Format:  21 ends duration
Variations:
(1)  Ends may vary according to local situation, e.g. league games/tournaments.

*Two accomplished Pairs specialists, Stephen Farish and Paul Barlow, who have won England National Outdoor and Indoor Pairs titles as well as the British Isles Outdoor Pairs. Stephen added the Pairs Silver Medal to his collection at the 2002 Commonwealth Games with his England partner Dean Morgan.*
(Courtesy of Bowls International)

*John Bell, Niall Currie and Ronnie Gass, winners of the 2007 Over 50 EIBA Triples title. This added to Bell's two National Outdoor Triples titles, one EIBA Triples title, a British Isles Outdoor title and a World Championship Triples Bronze Medal. Ronnie Gass and Niall Currie have been Scottish Outdoor Pairs winners, while Gass and Bell won the English National Outdoor Pairs.*
(© Trevor Costall)

*Cyphers Club Four: Terry Heppell, Martin Sekjer, Gary Smith and Andy Thomson. Arguably the best club four to compete in Britain, they have been prolific English and British Isles Fours Championship winners (outdoors and indoors).*
(Courtesy of Bowls International)

# CHAPTER 7

# POSITIONAL PLAY

## The Lead

Every position in team play has an important contribution to make. The lead, however, has an especially key role to play. He lays the foundation for every end, which his teammates can take advantage of and build on. He can and should be first to the jack. Good leading can make a massive contribution to winning games. On difficult surfaces a good lead bowl can often survive and remain shot right through the end. An in-form lead supported by an effective 'number two' player can wreak havoc on the opposition. This combination can take the opposition third out of the game, forcing him to play heavy retrieving shots. Such firefighting might save shots but seldom accrues them. Similarly the lead can exert pressure on the opposition second player.

The lead position in theory is a very attractive position. It is totally uncomplicated. The object is simple – you draw close to the jack. You have no bowls in your way and you don't have to worry about what weight to play. You need to master the speed of the green as quickly as possible and get on with drawing shots. This said, very few players crave to play there and indeed persist in the position. Those that do and master their craft are worth their weight in gold. Too many, however, find it boring or too difficult and long for the glory of the back-end players or the anonymity of the middle of the rink. Skipping in particular is perceived to be a much more glamorous and prestigious position. Others shy away from the lead position because of its exposed nature: leading with two bowls is not any easy task and if you happen to 'splay' them about a bit there is no place to hide! There is no doubt that it is a challenging position. It is, however, one

*John Ottaway, an exceptional England lead for over 20 years, including in the England Four who won the Commonwealth Games Gold Medal in 2002. He is also a three-time English Outdoor Singles winner.*
(Courtesy of Bowls International)

*Brett Morley, another brilliant lead for England – indoors and outdoors. He led in the successful gold medal-winning four at the World Championships in 1996. He has also won the English Outdoor Singles.*
(Courtesy of Bowls International)

that can bring a lot of personal satisfaction and one that, like the singles game, can greatly assist with your personal development in the game. If you become proficient at leading you will be an automatic choice in any team and able to take great pride in the fact that you are the 'bedrock' of team play.

## Guidelines for Leading

What do you need to do to develop your interest and skills in leading? The following will provide some guidance.

### Stick to Leading
If you have an aptitude for leading don't be coaxed away to play other positions. It is a specialist position – the more you play there, the more experience and confidence you will get. Leading with two bowls is not easy. You need to do it often. Too many bowlers who play with four bowls think it is just as easy to lead with two. It isn't. You have to focus more with two bowls. This will happen more naturally if you are leading with two bowls all the time. Similarly, when you play at the back end you are playing a wide variety of shots. You are not drawing continuously, which you are at lead. Don't complicate things. Stick to the job you have to do and make the lead position yours.

### Perfect the Art of Drawing
This is your sole objective, so make sure you are good at it. Very much like singles, you must draw consistently to the jack at all lengths, on varying surfaces and in all conditions.

### Jack and Mat
The outcome of games can often hinge on how successful you are in changing a jack length and/or the position of the mat. You need to be able to deliver the jack to wherever your skip directs you. It should waver no more than a metre from where he is standing.

### Select the Best Hands on the Rink
You must quickly assess the playing qualities of the rink, and choose the best

hands on which to play your bowls. Ideally you should try to play one side of the rink both ways. This will ensure that the pace of the green will be the same for each end and assist you in achieving a consistent length. When you have found a hand that is particularly suited to your play you should abandon it only if you are completely blocked out or need to play a specific shot on the other hand. Don't change simply because there is an opposition bowl on or near the line on your good hand. You will have a better chance of getting closer to the jack by sticking to that good hand and drawing past the obstructing bowl, than by changing to a bad hand that you are not playing regularly.

## Don't Be Short

Bowls that are more than 1m short are almost useless and contribute absolutely nothing to the building of a good head or covering back position. If you do fall short with your first bowl, make sure you are up to the head with your next. Never be short when shot is against you.

## Keep Involved

Once you deliver your bowls at lead it may be more than six or seven minutes before you play again. You must ensure you maintain your concentration. Encouraging and supporting your teammates certainly helps. Watching how the head builds up, and the ultimate outcome of the end, should also retain your attention and indeed assist with your knowledge of the game. You must, however, learn to condition yourself to focus fully again every time it is your turn to bowl. I know some leads who do this by treating their game against the opposing lead as a 'virtual singles' game. They mentally keep count of how many shots they have scored (or have scored against them) at each end. For example, if on end 1 a lead had his two bowls closer to the jack than his opponent he would score 2; if he kept doing this, at the end of the 21 ends he would win the virtual contest 42–0. I emphasize they only keep score in their heads, but it is an effective way to sharpen your competitive edge during the game.

*An accomplished exponent of the lead position, John Rednall has been British Isles Outdoor Pairs winner, bronze medallist in the fours in the World Championships in 2004, and English Indoor Singles champion.*
(Courtesy of Bowls International)

## Consult Your Skip

After the finish of each end consult your skip about the jack and mat tactics. Under the current rules, if your team wins the end you have the choice of delivering the jack to your chosen length, or giving the jack away, which gives your skip the advantage of playing the last bowl of the end. There are benefits and drawbacks to either course of action. If you give the jack away your opponents get to play at their favourite length. You, however, have the vital last bowl that has the 'last say' on the outcome of the end. Whatever the thinking, the lead must always ensure he consults with his skip before he delivers or gives away the jack.

Purposeful Practices for leads are shown in Figs 33, 34 and 35.

*The outstanding Scottish lead Sarah Gourlay has won the Commonwealth Games Pairs, Atlantic Rim Fours and Scottish Pairs twice.*
(Courtesy of Bowls International)

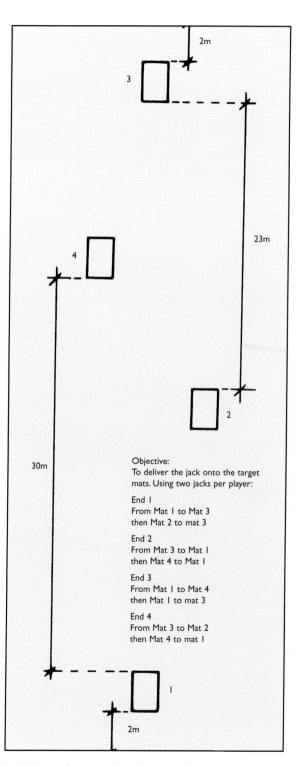

Objective:
To deliver the jack onto the target mats. Using two jacks per player:

End 1
From Mat 1 to Mat 3
then Mat 2 to mat 3

End 2
From Mat 3 to Mat 1
then Mat 4 to Mat 1

End 3
From Mat 1 to Mat 4
then Mat 1 to mat 3

End 4
From Mat 3 to Mat 2
then Mat 4 to mat 1

*Fig 33 Purposeful practice for leads – casting the jack.*

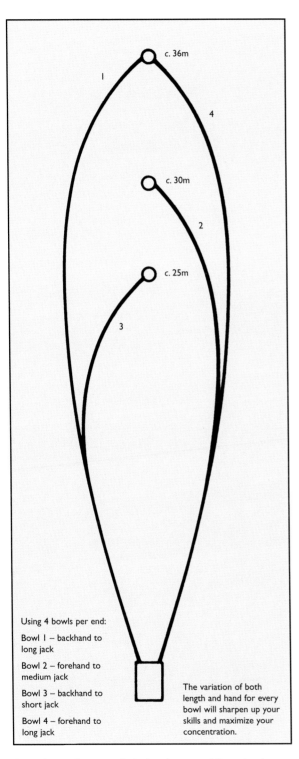

Using 4 bowls per end:

Bowl 1 – backhand to long jack

Bowl 2 – forehand to medium jack

Bowl 3 – backhand to short jack

Bowl 4 – forehand to long jack

The variation of both length and hand for every bowl will sharpen up your skills and maximize your concentration.

Fig 34  Purposeful practice for leads – drawing to different lengths.

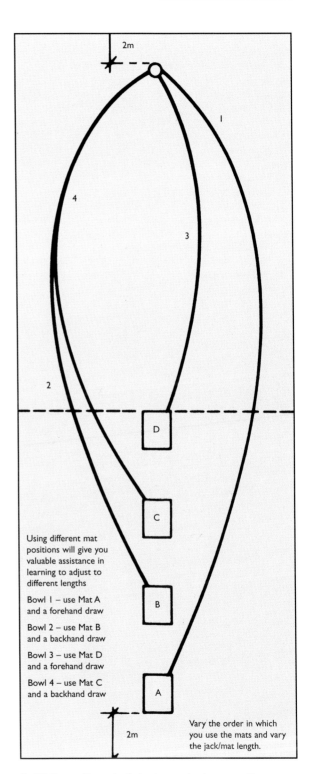

Using different mat positions will give you valuable assistance in learning to adjust to different lengths

Bowl 1 – use Mat A and a forehand draw

Bowl 2 – use Mat B and a backhand draw

Bowl 3 – use Mat D and a forehand draw

Bowl 4 – use Mat C and a backhand draw

Vary the order in which you use the mats and vary the jack/mat length.

Fig 35  Purposeful practice for leads – varying the mat position.

# The Second

This position at the heart of the team offers a wonderful opportunity for versatile players to express themselves. Nevertheless, its true value and purpose is quite often misunderstood and undervalued. It is viewed by many as the position in which to absorb a player – in other words, if you are to 'carry' a player, that's where it should be. Doubtless for this reason there is no shortage of volunteers to play there. In reality it is just the opposite. The number two has been described as the 'anchorman' of the rink. It is he who can make or break the position at the head. If your lead has done his job then your second player can consolidate that position and strengthen the head. If he hasn't, he can destroy and/or retrieve the position. If he fails, the problems continue through to the back-end play, with the advantage accruing to the opposition.

This role therefore demands a player with a wide range of shots at his disposal. It is predominantly a drawing position, but unlike the lead he does not have the luxury of a free run to the jack. The head will be starting to build in a positive or problematic fashion. If it is the latter, he may be called upon to play a weight shot, which may be anything from a metre on to a full-blooded drive, depending on the severity of the situation.

It is a truly fascinating position with a massive manipulative contribution to make and should never be undervalued.

## Guidelines for Seconds

There is some overlap with the playing attributes of a lead (for advice on selecting the best hands and involvement in the game, see above) but the basic requirements of good second play are set out below.

### Be Up to the Head
No player should be short, but this applies most definitely to the second player. His job is specifically to improve the head, whether that requires consolidation or retrieval. Short bowls will leave your team vulnerable, either in the head or at the back of the rink. Reaching the head must be your prime purpose, and you should be mentally prepared and conditioned to achieve that.

### Be Open-Minded
Your skip may call on you to play any of a number of shots, depending on the condition of the head. You must be prepared to play the necessary shot and be just as happy to drive at the head as you are to draw to it.

### Be Versatile
Concentrate on perfecting your draw, but ensure you practise your weight shots as well.

The second player also has the dubious honour of keeping the scorecard and filling in details of the scores after each end (for a typical scorecard, see Fig 5).

Purposeful Practices for Seconds are shown in Figs 21–23, 34 and 35.

## The Third

This is another position calling for a versatile player. The third can and should have a major influence on the outcome of the end. He can both seal ends up, so minimizing intervention by the opposition, as well as opening them up to create opportunities for his skip. The third must most definitely have all the shots at his disposal, particularly the really heavy ones. By the time the third is on the mat he could, in the most difficult

*World Indoor Singles champion and twice English Indoor Singles winner, Mervyn King is renowned as an exceptional team player, excelling at Number 2 in various English representative sides.*
(Courtesy of Bowls International)

circumstances, have six shots against him with both drawing hands blocked. His drive therefore could be crucial to destroying the head or at least opening it up for his skip. Equally he may be six shots down with an open hand and he must draw the shot. He must expect to play all the shots during a game, and he must be able to execute them all effectively.

A third's greatest strength should be his ability to relate positively to his skip. He is the skip's loyal lieutenant. He must support him, take pressure off him and bring out the best in him. The ability to do this will often win games. If you produce the right blend at the back end of a rink it can be a formidable force.

## Guidelines for Thirds

A good third needs to be proficient in the full range of shots, but he should also possess other special attributes. He should exert, to the best of his abilities, a positive influence on the rest of the team, particularly the skip.

### Respect for the Skip
Whatever decisions the skip makes in relation to his directions to his team, or his own individual choice of shot, they must always be enthusiastically accepted and supported. There is absolutely no place for dissent and disagreement. I have seen so many situations in which the third considers that he is better than his skip, and thinks he should be skipping instead. His general demeanour, and sometimes his antagonistic relationship with his skip, instantly destroys team spirit and harmony, and actually gives a boost to the opposition. The team's performance usually deteriorates as a result. A good third is totally flexible and blends with the wishes and style of his skip.

### Awareness
A third should be aware of the styles of himself and his skip, and ensure they are compatible.

### Motivating the Skip
If you know how to motivate your skip and bring out the best in him you are a long way down the road to success. He has the final bowls to play at each end. He must make optimum use of them. If he is fired up and knows he has the genuine support of his team he will respond accordingly. A good third will orchestrate this necessary support.

### Clear Communication
Some skips like regular updates from the head, others don't. Communication must serve a useful purpose. In general terms keep it to a minimum, unless otherwise instructed. Gratuitous comments only serve to irritate.

### Providing the Link
You must make your front end feel involved and listen to their suggestions regarding tactics and ideas, feeding them through to the skip at the appropriate moment – if he hasn't already taken them into account.

Purposeful Practices and Shots for Thirds are illustrated in Figs 21–24, 34 and 37.

*Robert Newman, the talented and accomplished Number 3 player, won the Fours Gold Medal in the 2002 Commonwealth Games and Bronze Medal at the 2004 World Championships. He has now progressed to become an established international skip.*
*(Courtesy of Bowls International)*

## The Skip

The skip has the most important role in every team discipline – pairs, triples and fours. He is in total control of the team play and dictates all the tactics involved. He may very likely consult with his players in this respect, but he will have the last say. The best skips are normally accomplished bowlers with extensive experience and many notable achievements. A good skip is the ultimate bowling craftsman. He can play all the shots with great effect and will have played in every position during his career, which gives him intimate knowledge of the particular skills required for each. This is invaluable when directing his players in those positions. He will be well respected and his players will have the utmost confidence in his ability. His achievements and his management of his team will have earned that respect.

Traditionally, however, it is not uncommon for club officials and/or the oldest subscribing members to skip at club level as a reward for their contributions to the club. On the other hand, many modern skips have been fast-tracked through the system after showing promise in other positions. They have then been elevated to the skipping position owing to a general shortage of capable players in the club. This is undoubtedly an honour, and welcome recognition to an aspiring bowler, but beware. Always remember there is a big difference between a good bowler playing last, and a good skip. There is no substitute for experience, which ideally includes a meaningful apprenticeship served under a good skip who has earned that responsibility, and not under one who has been self-appointed or fast-tracked. Skipping involves more than the art of bowling. A good skip needs to be a 'people manager' too, ensuring that he gets the best out of his players.

Despite that, I fully understand and admire any talented bowler whose ambition is focused on becoming a recognized skip. And I certainly would not wish to discourage him. One of the biggest honours you can achieve in bowls is to be picked for your country as skip. It is recognition that you have become the complete bowler: not only can you play the best bowls, you can be entrusted with the task of managing three other top bowlers, and leading them to success. The same principles apply to selections as skip in county and national competition.

My point, however, is that you must learn your trade properly. Look and learn. I will identify below what I consider to be the key elements in the make-up of a good skip. The theory alone is not enough. You need to experience it being applied at first hand in the company of good, established skips. Playing with or against a good skip is ideal. If this is not possible, make a point of going to watch one of the recognized skips in your area. If you are a talented bowler, possess personal leadership skills and are

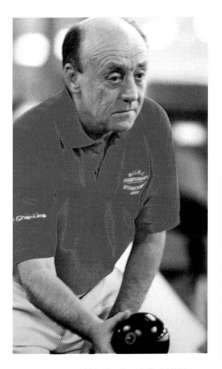

The charismatic Welsh skip David (Dai) Wilkins, who has been one of the most competitive and revered skips in the British Isles.
(Courtesy of Bowls International)

The legendary skip Willie Wood MBE has played for Scotland for more than 40 years and is still one of the top skips in the British Isles.
(Courtesy of Bowls International)

willing to learn, there is no reason you cannot graduate to the ultimate level of responsibility in bowls and become one of the 'bowling samurai' – the trusted skip.

## Guidelines for Skipping

### Tactical Control
From start to finish you must be in total control of your team's tactical play, right from directing the lead where to throw the jack and where to place the mat. Tell your players which hand to play, what weight to play and where you want their bowls to finish.

### Be Alert
You must be perceptive and alert. You must be able to read the head, know when to build it, when to protect it and when to attack it. You must be astute enough to reassess the situation in the event of unexpected developments during an end. You must not be caught out by failing to respond to vulnerable situations, for example when there are no back bowls or there is only one bowl in the head.

### Know Your Team
You must be fully aware of the strengths and weaknesses of your own players. This will influence the shots you ask them to play

### Assess Your Opponents
You must also quickly assess the strengths and weaknesses of your opponents. You

*Mary Price, the world-class English skip. Her many titles include the World and UK Singles and the Australian International Mixed Pairs with the author.*
(Courtesy of Bowls International)

can then dictate play in a way that exposes their weaknesses and limits their opportunity to show their strengths: if, for example, the opposition lead and second are obviously struggling at a long length then you will ask your lead to throw long jacks.

### Assess the Green
You must quickly assess the playing qualities of the green, in order to direct your players onto the good hands and easier lengths.

### Leadership
You must develop and demonstrate good leadership skills. These will improve with experience. You must be able to motivate your teammates and keep them fully involved in the game. You must encourage them by verbally congratulating them, shaking hands or slapping them on the back when they play a good bowl. Never, never ignore them. There is nothing more soul destroying for a player than to be trying his heart out only to be ignored. He will be turned off and his performance will deteriorate. Equally, be sympathetic when a poor bowl is played by one of your team. A skip should always be positive and helpful, never destructive. Avoid sarcastic comments. Nobody likes to be humiliated. Only if you know your players really well can you engage in some humorous and/or sarcastic remark in the knowledge they can laugh at the comment along with you. There are lots of ways to make a point about a poor bowl without upsetting anyone. This is an art the skip must master. Never turn your back on a bad bowl; this has the same effect, if not worse, than a critical remark. You must develop a good rapport with your teammates, on and off the green. You play the game as a unit and socialize as a unit afterwards. There should be no public witch-hunts. A privately conducted debriefing after the game is very constructive. It is good for the whole unit to analyse where the game was won or lost, and who contributed and who failed at certain ends. A public witch-hunt, on the other hand, is totally demoralizing and counterproductive to good future performances. Each player knows how he's

played after a game. If someone has had a bad game the last thing he wants is to be publicly identified as the 'man who lost the match'. A private word from the skip on what he thinks went wrong and how it can be rectified next time is far more helpful and constructive.

### Confidence
You must be confident, positive and upbeat. You must lead by example and make sure you keep the spirits of your players up when your team is being beaten. Never let your head drop: both the opposition and your own players will sense you are worried and losing confidence. You must also be decisive with the choice of shot you play, and with the shots you direct your players to play. Never get caught in two minds or you will invariably fail in your objective. When you stand on the mat you must be sure and confident about the shot you are going to play. You will often consult your teammates on the choice of shot, particularly your third, but try to avoid long and protracted 'committee meetings' about which shot to play. In my experience these do more to confuse the skip than help him choose the right shot, and it certainly disrupts the rhythm of the game.

### Pressure
You must be able to withstand pressure. You are the last line of defence for your four, and perhaps for a whole team. You will be called upon to play the most difficult of shots under intense scrutiny. You must remain calm and focused, and rise to any occasion that may occur. You must be the 'iceman' of your side.

### Communication
You must be a good communicator, issuing clear and concise instructions to your players in a manner that will maximize their contribution. The better you know your players the more effective you will be at this aspect.

### Shot Selection
You must be particularly adept at shot selection. You have the unenviable job of balancing all the relevant considerations –

speed of the green, quality of the hands, the weather (if outdoors), the position at the head, the capabilities of your players and those of your opponent – against what shot to play. This is a particular skill that can only be developed through experience. Nevertheless, a good skip will always utilize the 'percentage' shot wherever he can. This is the shot that will give you the most chances of success. It is particularly effective outdoors where there are more variations in the lines to the jack caused by idiosyncrasies in the surface, for example when a situation might give a 'yard on' shot a better percentage chance of getting shot than a neat draw.

## Summary

Skipping is not an easy position, yet play it well and there is enormous satisfaction to be had. Skips have the most influence over winning games. It is indeed a prestigious position, but good skips are not made overnight. They need to evolve responsibly and carefully. The successful development of our great game needs a continuous supply of good skips coming through the ranks to take the helm at all levels. Aspiring skips need to be continually recognized and developed in a way that endows them with both the necessary skills and understanding of what it takes to become one of bowls' finest. It is important, however, to recognize the difference between true skips and impostors. Not everyone has the necessary make-up to succeed at skip, but that does not mean you cannot make a significant contribution elsewhere. It is important you analyse your own capabilities and limitations and concentrate on the position to which you are best suited, and where you can make the most significant contribution to winning the game. You could be an excellent shot player but have an awful personality, a great draw bowler but can't drive, or a great all-round player but hate pressure. There is a guaranteed place in a side for you, but not necessarily at skip.

For those of you with the potential and determination to fulfil the role of a skip in its fullest sense as outlined above – then the glory and pride of the 'bowling samurai' await you.

*David Ward, the long-serving and accomplished English skip (1982–97), played with nerves of steel, and represented England at the Edinburgh Commonwealth Games.*
*(Courtesy of Bowls International)*

*Capturing his numerous British and English titles as skip, Tony Allcock MBE was skip of the winning English four in the World Outdoor Championships. He also skipped David Bryant (five times), David Holt (once) and Mervyn King (once) to seven World Indoor Pairs victories. He is an excellent communicator and tactician, and a skilled exponent of the percentage shot.*
*(Courtesy of Bowls International)*

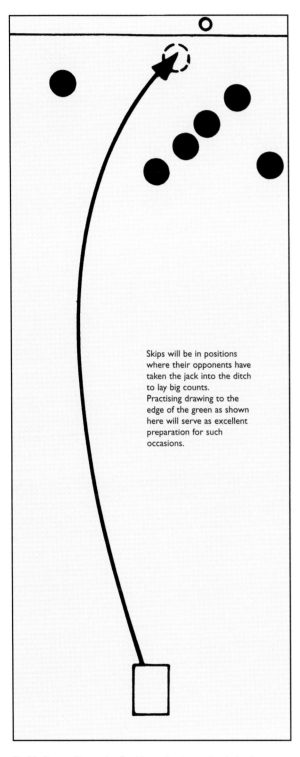

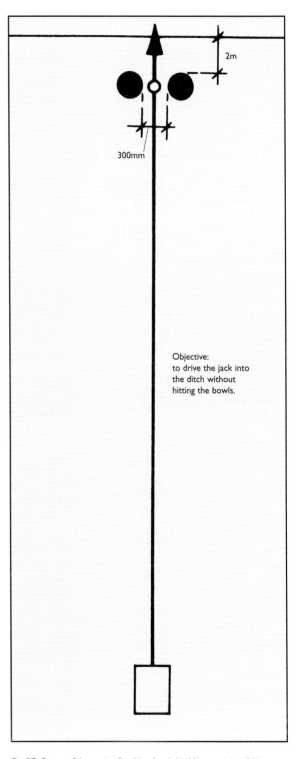

*Fig 36 Purposeful practice for skips – drawing to the ditch edge.*

*Fig 37 Purposeful practice for skips (and thirds) – precision driving.*

Purposeful Practices for Skips are shown in Figs 36 and 37 (for other appropriate shots for skips to practise, see Figs 10, 21–26).

# The Officials

Let us now look at the main officials in the game. It will be useful for you to have an insight into the roles and duties of the markers and umpires who officiate in singles games and in the various competitions and matches you will be involved with. This will enable you to understand how and why they operate during the matches. It will also familiarize you with what is required should you be asked to act as a marker, as indeed you invariably will be. It may be that at some point you wish to consider becoming a qualified umpire yourself, whereupon an early sight of the duties involved will also be of value.

By the very nature of the official positions of marker and umpire, it is important the duties involved are carried out properly. Their decisions and actions can greatly influence the outcome of games. Giving the correct advice and undertaking crucial measures in a competent and tactful manner is an essential requirement for these officials.

Under these circumstances I feel it wise to ensure you are fully aware of all the exact official duties involved. I have therefore (with the kind permission of World Bowls Ltd) reproduced the duties as they are set out in the Laws of the Sport.

## The Marker's Duties

The marker is engaged to officiate during a game of singles. He sees that the game is played in accordance with the Laws of the Sport.

1  In the absence of an umpire, the marker should:
   • make sure that all aspects of play are carried out in line with the Laws of the Sport of Bowls;

Umpires inspecting bowls at the EIBA National Championships held at Northampton Indoor Bowls Club. (© John Bell)

- check, before the game starts, that: all bowls have a clearly visible, valid World Bowls Stamp imprinted on them; the rink of play is the correct width in line with law 5.1 by measuring it; and the pegs or discs on the side banks in the direction of play are the correct distances in line with law 5.12 by measuring them.

2 The marker should:
- centre the jack;
- check that the jack is at least 23 metres from the mat line after it has been centred;
- place a jack that comes to rest less than 2 metres from the front ditch as described in law 22.2;
- stand to one side of the rink, behind the jack and away from the head;
- answer any specific question about the state of the head which is asked by the player in possession of the rink;
- when asked, tell or show the player in possession of the rink the position of the jack;
- when asked, tell or show the player in possession of the rink which bowl or bowls the marker considers to be shot;
- when authorized by the Controlling Body, signal to players and spectators (using the appropriate number and colour of shot indicators or some other suitable method) which player's bowl or bowls the marker considers to be shot;
- mark all touchers with chalk and remove the chalk marks from non-touchers as soon as they come to rest;
- if both players agree, remove all dead bowls from the rink of play;

- mark the position of the jack and any touchers which are in the ditch as described in laws 24.4 and 29.2;
- not move, or cause to be moved, either the jack or any bowls until the players have agreed the number of shots scored; and
- measure any disputed shot or shots when asked to do so by either player. If the players are not satisfied with the marker's decision, the marker should ask the umpire to do the measuring. If the Controlling Body has not appointed an umpire, the marker should choose a competent neutral person to act as the umpire. The umpire's decision is final.

3 When each end has been completed, the marker should:
- record the score on the score card;
- tell the players the running totals of the scores; and
- remove from the rink the mat used during the previous end, if necessary.

4 When the game has been completed, the marker should make sure that the score card:
- contains the names and signatures of the players;
- contains the time at which the game was completed; and
- is dealt with in line with the Conditions of Play.

## The Umpire's Duties

The umpire has overall authority over any game, competition or tournament he is overseeing. He has total responsibility for enforcing the Laws of the Sport.

1 An umpire should be appointed by, or on behalf of, the Controlling Body for the competition.

2 The umpire's duties are as follows. To check, before the games starts, that:
- all bowls have a clearly visible, valid World Bowls Stamp imprinted on them;
- the rink of play is the correct width in line with law 5.1 by measuring it; and
- the pegs or discs on the side banks in the direction of play are the correct distances in line with law 5.12 by measuring them.
- The umpire should measure any disputed shot or shots using suitable measuring equipment, such as that described in law 10.
- The umpire should decide whether the distance of the mat from the rear and front ditches and the distance of the jack or a bowl from the mat line are in line with the Laws of the Sport of Bowls or not.
- The umpire should decide whether a jack or a bowl is in play or not.
- The umpire should make sure that all aspects of play are in line with the Laws of the Sport of Bowls.
- The umpire's decision is final in all circumstances except those relating to the meaning or interpretation of a law, in which case there will be a right of appeal to the Controlling Body.

The Laws of the Sport of Bowls in full, along with the objectives and functions of World Bowls Ltd, can be viewed on their website, www.worldbowlsltd.co.uk.

# CHAPTER 8

# PLAYING WITH CONFIDENCE

Confidence is a key factor in achieving success at any sport. It has a particularly important part to play in bowls and you must learn how to both gain it and retain it.

Confidence brings a sense of reassurance and optimism to your game. It is fundamental to ensuring you take a positive and disciplined approach to the various situations you will be faced with during a game. It thrives on experience and success. Careful shot selection followed by the perfect execution of that shot gives a tremendous boost to your confidence along with a warm feeling of satisfaction. Do this repeatedly and your confidence grows and grows, which in turn has a very beneficial effect on your performance. The doubts you may have about your ability begin to disappear – negative thoughts are replaced by positive and clear thinking. The object is to develop and maintain this confident approach.

Gwyn John, former National Director of Coaching and an astute scholar of bowling technique, fully acknowledges the importance of a confident approach. He states that confidence is not a random feeling. It is normally gained as a result of application, hard work and honesty. The only shortcut is an abundance of natural ability. For the majority, however, it is a question of getting down to it and working hard at those areas of the game that we realize need to be improved.

Situations, of course, will occur that conspire to undermine your confidence. It may be an unlucky result from a perfectly

played bowl by yourself, or an extremely lucky result from a badly played bowl by your opponent. It could be that continual driving shots from your opponent constantly destroy your perfect draw shots. You must be strong. 'Good sound confidence', says Gwyn John, 'comes from within and under no circumstances should it be shaken by anything that happens during a game.' There is a need to be determined and not to be upset – not to drop your head, but to remain 'calm and in control'.

You cannot control the uncontrollable, but there is everything you yourself can do to produce your best bowling. You are in charge. It is you who must demonstrate you are confident and in control, to allow your concentration and consistency to be employed to the full. Do so and you will be able to play to the best of your potential.

## Self-Control

Self-control can have a major influence on your confidence. The following pointers should help to retain your confidence and minimize the chances of it being undermined.

- Always keep calm and remain positive when under pressure;
- Concentrate only on the relevant issues affecting the situation;
- Be absolutely clear on the shot you are

going to play when you are in trouble – don't be caught in two minds;
- Try to be as relaxed as possible and don't rush your shot(s);
- Make sure you are always aware of the position at the head.

## Temperament

Temperament is another major influence on confidence and can be instrumental in winning you games. Whatever personality you have developed in life, you must shape your behaviour and attitude on the bowling green in a way that gives you the best chance of achieving success.

- You must have the ability to play your best at crucial times in the games;
- You must not be disheartened by shots – lucky or unlucky – played by the opposition, or unlucky results suffered by yourself;
- You must have the determination and resilience to battle on in the face of all adversity. You must never give up, even if the situation appears to be irretrievable;
- You must approach every game in a positive frame of mind. I know you will say that is all very good in theory, but how can you be positive when you are a club four and are about to play a four made up of international players. Well, you must still remain positive. If the game is outdoors the vagaries of the greens can often prove a great leveller and a positive result is always possible. In any case there are other positive ways in which you can approach the game. Set your stall out to make it the best game you have played. Use it to set yourself new personal standards, so ensuring you get something out of the game. Your overall game will undoubtedly improve as a result.

*Jamie Chestney is an exemplar of confident youth, becoming a valued member of both the England Senior Indoor and Outdoor teams at the tender age of 20.*
(Courtesy of Bowls International)

# CHAPTER 9

# PLAYING ON DIFFERENT SURFACES

*Jim Baker, World Indoor Singles champion and World Outdoor Triples and Fours winner, is celebrated as one of Britain's most talented and exciting skips of his era on both indoor and outdoor surfaces.*
(Courtesy of Bowls International)

## Outdoor Greens

Between April and September you will be able to enjoy a short and intensive season of outdoor bowls. In that time you will experience a variety of grass greens, the pace and playing characteristics of which can change by the hour. Wind and rain, a rare hot spell, the length of the grass, minor variations of level: these all influence the way in which your bowl reacts on the rink. You will find no two rinks alike; one rink may even play differently in the afternoon to how it plays in the morning. A rain-soaked green in the morning will usually produce narrow running lines to the jack. When it dries out the hands will become bigger, requiring a wider line to the jack.

While there is no better way to enjoy our great game of bowls than playing outdoors on a free-running green in glorious sunshine, I also know that outdoor greens can pose many playing problems for us all. Frustrating though it may be at times, it is all part and parcel of the outdoor game. It adds to the challenge and indeed the satisfaction when we 'unlock' a green's many secrets. You will, however, quickly appreciate that reading the green well is a necessary skill to add to your list of 'must haves' if you wish to succeed at the game. It is essential that

---

**USEFUL TIP**

When playing outdoors always take into account any peculiarities of the rink when choosing your shot. Avoid the difficult hands. Vary the length of the jack and position of the mat until you find a jack length that responds best to your bowls and style of play.

you learn to identify the good hands – never waste bowls on hands that don't allow your bowl to bend. You must quickly work out if one side of the green is running faster than the other. Is the green playing faster in one direction than the other? (I know many greens that are on a slight incline.) If the wind starts to blow, how much is it affecting the bowls? Does the rink play differently at certain lengths? The grass might be shorter in one area of the rink, in which case the bowls will run faster on it. You need to be alert to all these factors should they occur. Playing conditions dictate your choice of shot far more on the outdoor surface than indoors. In the indoor game it is nearly always possible to draw around bowls, owing to the faster running surface and wide drawing nature of the hands. Outdoors the heavy nature of the green, together with the narrow nature of the hands, will often not allow it. In these circumstances the 'yard on' percentage shot is often very appropriate, particularly for back-end players.

---

**USEFUL TIP**

Get your coach to demonstrate the variations that can occur because of the conditions on the outdoor green (the straight runs, the difference of pace and so on) and to assist you to identify the symptoms quickly. After the rinks have been played on and the games have finished, for example, create a new rink by moving the rink markers across by half a rink width. This will produce a rink that has one side that has been previously played on and one that hasn't. Experience the variation of pace between the two hands.

---

## Choice of Bowl

The generally heavy nature of outdoor greens, along with their associated narrow lines, also influences the type of bowl you play with. As a general rule you would be well advised to use a set of bowls with at least a medium bias, which have the ability

*Betty Morgan MBE, the Welsh outdoor specialist, played in the Welsh outdoor team for 29 years and has won 26 Welsh Outdoor titles and 11 British Isles Outdoor titles.*
*(Courtesy of Bowls International)*

to bend around short bowls and react positively to narrow hands. Leads may get away with a narrower running bowl as they normally have a free run at the jack, but even so, if they come to play in singles or other occasional positions, a very narrow running bowl will reduce your shot options when there are more bowls in the head.

It is also important to ensure that your bowls are dry and manageable. When you play outdoors it is not uncommon to experience cold and wet conditions. These will affect your grip. It is essential you ensure the surface of your bowl is never impaired or slippery. You need full control of your bowls and your grip must not be hampered by dampness or pieces of earth or grass. You must always use a cloth to dry and clean your bowls in wet conditions. I would even go further and strongly recommend you use one of the many gripping agents that are available to smear on the bowls to give them a somewhat 'sticky' feel. This I find extremely helpful in improving control and avoiding any slippage in the hand.

Cold and wet conditions can also expose another problem – playing with bowls that are too big for you. Always ensure you have bowls that you can fully control in all conditions.

## Delivery

The various conditions experienced in outdoor bowls will pose many interesting challenges, but you must retain faith in the basic mechanics of the stance and delivery action that you have adopted and developed. You need to maintain the delivery action you have practised and you must not change it in an effort to overcome problems of the playing surface. If, for example, a bowl needs to be delivered down a narrow line (and it often does) then look to the placing of your feet on the mat. Never forget you have the full width of the mat to use. Step across the mat and stand on the edge of it in order for you to achieve a tighter line or to bowl inside a short bowl. Remember, you must have one foot on or above the mat at the point of delivery in order to conform to the Laws of the Sport.

There is also a question of weight. Bowlers need to ensure they reach the head in heavy conditions. The most important factor in achieving this is by increasing the speed of the bowling arm. Any such acceleration must, however, be controlled in order to retain good balance when the bowl is delivered. If you try to increase the speed of your bowl by flinging your body forward it will result in you losing body balance. This must be retained at all times. Some bowlers may benefit from adopting a more upright stance to increase the momentum of their movement. If this is the case, then you must ensure you do not step forward too far. This will seriously disjoint your movement and usually results in the bowl being lobbed out of your hand instead of being smoothly delivered at grass level.

*No need for sweaters at the 2006 Commonwealth Games in Melbourne! England's Pairs Silver Medallists – Ian Bond and Mark Bantock – are congratulated by their Team Manager, John Bell.*

## Dress

You must ensure you are well prepared for outdoor weather conditions with a range of warm tops of various thicknesses and, of course, the faithful wet suit. However, also make sure these articles of clothing allow you the necessary freedom of movement to undertake your normal delivery action. Two or three layers of clothing, an undersized waterproof top or trousers, or a garment with sleeves that are too short, can all have a detrimental effect on your delivery.

---

**USEFUL TIP**

When buying your various items of bowling attire, make sure you go through your delivery action with them on before you buy, in order to ensure you have the necessary freedom of movement.

---

## Indoor Greens

Indoor surfaces are completely different from the 'great outdoors'. They are faster and much more consistent in terms of the conditions experienced. The pace of an indoor green may change during a game, but never to the same extent as its outdoor counterpart. Temperature change can sometimes affect the surface tension of the carpet: an end rink adjacent to an entry/exit point, for example, can sometimes be cooled by outside air, resulting in a slightly slower pace. On a cold frosty morning the cooler atmosphere in the stadium can result in a slower pace to that when the heating has warmed the building through.

Indoor bowls is a very different game to the outdoor one. Faster and truer indoor surfaces produce closer heads to bowl to. It is easier to drive more accurately. There are fewer variables to contend with indoors and it is technically easier to play there. Reading the green is also a lot easier. Of course, there are variations between rinks but they are all

*Greg Harlow, the indoor specialist, has been three times back-to-back winner of the International Open Indoor Singles and England's most consistent indoor singles player at recent televised events.*
*(Courtesy of Bowls International)*

generally wide-lined, where the golden rule is never 'under green' your bowl. You will not get away with a narrow bowl – you will normally be punished by finishing well inside the head and out of the game. Tactically, too, the closer heads need better protection. The 'block' and the back positional bowl take on an even more important role indoors, while the 'yard on shot', a fundamental strength in the outdoor game, is a difficult and less effective shot on the quicker bending indoor surfaces.

The quicker pace and bigger bends of the indoor surfaces generally demand the closest attention. You must concentrate on your weight control and delivery lines in particular. Minor errors at delivery are magnified significantly by the quick running and big bending nature of the indoor surfaces. You will need to adjust your outdoor delivery to cope with these conditions.

## Delivery

Assuming you have developed a competent delivery action for outdoor play, you will need to make minor but essential adjustments to it for indoor games. You will look to:

- develop a shorter backswing with the bowling arm;
- a slower transference of bodyweight forward;
- a slower follow through of the bowling arm.

You might find that bending your knees a little more will assist in reducing the forward momentum. In essence you need to slow your whole delivery movement down until it adjusts to the weight of the carpet. You will soon find out if your delivery action is too quick, because you will invariably bowl with too much weight and finish well past the head. The less movement involved with your delivery, the better you will handle the quicker surfaces. Once again practice very much makes perfect, and practice in the company of a qualified coach will help you to make the necessary adjustments faster.

## Choice of Bowl

The bowl you use indoors must be able to respond effectively to the characteristics of the playing surface. You must take full advantage of your home surface, where you will be playing the majority of your games. The size of bowl indoors is not as critical as it is outdoors. However, it must be comfortable and capable of being fully controlled. Interestingly, with regard to grip, you may consider using the cradle grip indoors as another means of adjusting better to the faster carpets. The claw grip provides a better means of propelling the bowl on heavy outdoor greens, but this is counterproductive indoors. You will soon discover which works best for you in your practice sessions.

The weight of the bowl is also an important consideration indoors. You have the choice of medium or heavy. Most top players use heavyweight bowls because they counter the wide arcs required and produce a more regular line, which is less demanding (the wider the line the bigger margin for error there is terms of weight and length). You must, however, assess the pros and cons of the various types of bowl against the characteristics of the playing surface to be played on. Generally speaking the faster the surface the more suited it will be to a heavier, narrower bending bowl. A big biased medium-weight bowl will not be suitable for a fast, bending green. It will, for example, prevent you from playing the outside hand of an end rink. The line you would need to take would be beyond the side ditch and any line inside that would result in you always finishing well inside the jack line.

There are now numerous sets of bowls available with varying biases. You should try them out in order to get a set that suits both your playing needs and the indoor surface. Always remember you still need to bend round bowls and on an indoor surface it is almost always possible to do that, but don't reduce your chances by using too narrow bending bowls (unless you intend to be an out and out lead).

## Other Useful Considerations

### Tiredness
Playing long periods in an indoor stadium can be very tiring. Refresh yourself by taking a breath of fresh air outside at regular intervals.

### Lighting
Many bowlers find that the artificial lighting can be distracting, in which case wearing a visor can help to reduce, or block out, the glare.

### Mat Lengths
Make sure you have early practice at different mat lengths. This will enable you to adjust to the varying aiming points required. Use the mat with confidence. Adjusting to different jack lengths indoors is harder than in the outdoor game. Vary your lengths in practice to ensure you are not caught out during competition.

# CHAPTER 10

# TOP TIPS

I hope that by now I have given a comprehensive picture of how you can learn, and develop, the skills and knowledge to play bowls successfully and enjoyably.

I will conclude with a selection of 'top tips' that reflect and enhance the advice I have offered throughout this book. These reflect the views of many top players and coaches, not least my dear departed friend Jimmy Davidson – bowls visionary, former National Coach, fellow TV commentator and International player; Mal Hughes – soul mate and motivator, fellow TV commentator, International Skip and former England Team Manager; and Tony

Allcock, David Bryant and Andy Thomson – good friends, World Championship-winning colleagues and three of the best players the world of bowls has ever seen.

## Practice

### Benefits

Never underestimate the benefit of practice. Make the most of your potential by dedicated and purposeful practice. It can and will make the difference between

victory and defeat. Use a coach to help you make it more effective and enjoyable through the introduction of a variety of competitive elements.

### Target Your Sessions

Gear your practice sessions to your immediate needs: remedying a particular delivery problem, reading the weight of the green better or preparing yourself for a specific position. If you are playing lead in your next game, for example, you may want to practise delivering the jack to set

*Mal Hughes, Jimmy Davidson and John Bell taking a break from commentating for the BBC at the World Indoor Championships in Preston Guild Hall.*
*(© John Bell)*

*Andy Thomson, a true world-class champion and three times winner of the World Indoor Singles title, four times English Indoor Singles winner, World Championship Fours winner in Adelaide and a prolific winner of other English and British titles.*
(Courtesy of Bowls International)

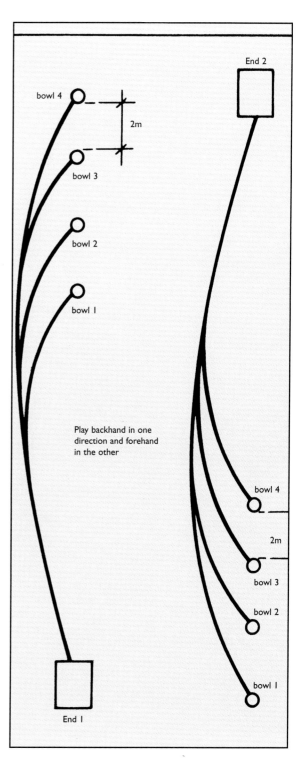

Fig 38  Purposeful practice for adjusting your weight.

lengths, and varying the mat position during play. Never just roll bowls up without setting yourself particular objectives for your practice sessions.

## Judging Speed

Practice sessions can be particularly useful for learning to read the speed of the green and how the weight can vary between the hands and in the two directions. In doing this you may find it useful to keep the jack length constant for a number of ends.

## Adjusting Your Weight

Practice too can greatly assist you in learning to adjust your weight (see Fig 38). Playing consecutively to a line of four jacks placed 2m apart can be of great benefit. With your first bowl, start drawing to the nearest one, then draw to the next jack with your second bowl and so on. Play all your four bowls on the backhand during this end. Then at the next end play your forehand, drawing first to the jack furthest away from you and work back towards you with your next three deliveries. Vary the length of the jacks during your practice.

## Prepare for the Unexpected

Make sure you practise playing to the jack in abnormal positions – draw to off-centre jacks near the boundaries of the rink and to off-centre jacks in the ditch. This will ensure you get used to selecting lines that are off the 'normal track', and it will also familiarize you with situations that don't arise too often in a game. Practise them and they will not take you by surprise in a proper game.

## Work on Your Weaknesses

Play the hands and lengths that you try to avoid in a competitive match. You must be competent at all lengths and with both your forehand and backhand. Build your confidence in practice.

## Seek Advice

Seek the advice and guidance of a qualified coach to assist you in making the most of your practice. They are there for your benefit. In particular, don't be afraid to seek help about any aspect of your delivery. I watch so many deliveries that produce bowls that are bounced and wobbled. In most cases a purposeful practice session could rectify these problems by simple and minimal adjustments to the grip or stance.

# Playing the Game

## Preparation

Work out a personal strategy for your preparation before a game so that you are relaxed, focused and positive. Whatever that may involve, make sure you always arrive in good time before a game and that you never have to rush right onto the green to play.

## Keep It Simple

Don't complicate things. The easier shot is usually the right one.

## Reacting on the Day

Plan to play to your strengths and your opponents' weaknesses, but learn too to react to the circumstances and conditions on the day. You may find you are scoring at certain lengths simply because your opponent is worse than you: the bowls may not be close, but you are finding it better than him. Try to keep that length. Remember that playing a mediocre game but scoring is better than playing well and not.

## Scoring with the Draw

Master the draw shot – the vast majority of scoring shots are drawn to the jack. Don't become addicted to the driving

shot. It has a valuable role to play, but must be used with discretion. The draw shot is required by every position played, so make sure you are good at it.

## Watch the Back

Don't lose silly shots by ignoring the position against you at the back of the rink. Always try to cover any accumulation of opposition bowls.

## Build the Head

Always ensure you have more than one bowl in the head. Build the head early. This will increase your shot options later.

## Short Bowls

Never be consistently short. Short bowls are the scourge of the game, and are the biggest single factor determining the outcome of a game. Short bowls lose games!

## Touchers

Respond to an opposition toucher by trying to get your next bowl as close as possible. It will reduce the chances of your opponent scoring another shot, and it will increase your own shot options.

## Positive Play

Don't be negative. While it is unwise to play heavy bowls all the time, it is better to be positive than too cautious, particularly when playing at the back end of a rink. If it is possible to draw do so, but don't be too tentative, and if the hands are difficult to negotiate make sure you attack the head.

## Decisions, Decisions …

Don't be caught in two minds. Work out your shot options, select the best one and play it positively. If you are still mentally deciding whether to draw or drive you will play an in-between shot and miss the line.

## Keep it Tight

If both hands are equally true then choose the tighter hand. It should be the easier hand to play.

## Trial Ends

Make the best use of your trial ends in competitive games. Watch, and learn from *all* the bowls being played. Stand behind the centre line if you can.

# Team Spirit

## Support Each Other

Show open and full support for your playing partners. Engage in positive encouragement and appreciation. Shaking hands, a slap on the back and a word of confidence, such as 'you can get this', can all be great motivators.

## Avoid Criticism

Never openly criticize your teammates. Never turn your back on any of their bowls as a mark of disgust, and don't provide unnecessary or gratuitous information, such as 'you're narrow', 'you're not up' or 'you're heavy again'. These are the biggest turn-offs in the game.

## Hide Your Feelings

Never allow the opposition to see that you are worried or rattled. Be careful your body language doesn't give you away: miserable faces and frustrated gestures can inspire opponents. The game, as they say, is never over until 'the fat lady sings'. Quite often she might be clearing her throat, but also quite often she can be prevented from singing by a spirited fightback.

## Working as a Team

A good four/triple/pair know each others' strengths and weaknesses and play the appropriate tactical game to suit. If the situation allows it, let the player play the shot he fancies.

## Communication

Always communicate instructions and information clearly and concisely. Support your vocal advice with hand signals to indicate distances, hands and shots held.

# Self-Control

## Concentration

In team games, particularly the fours, you will only spend a small percentage of the game delivering your bowls. Make sure you retain and maximize your concentration at these precious moments. Ensure you are not still engaged in conversation when you go to the mat. You must totally focus on the job in hand, playing and understanding the shot you are required to play.

## Positive Thinking

### Look Ahead
Ignore the bad bowls you have played. The only bowl that should be in your mind is the next one, especially if the last one you played was poor. Positive thoughts about future bowls are essential. Never allow fear of failure to enter your mind when you're on the mat: 'Failure thrives on a mind that fears it', as Jimmy Davidson used to say. Avoid thinking about the consequences of missing. Concentrate instead on the mechanics of the shot rather than the outcome.

### Ignore the Uncontrollables
Never let the 'uncontrollables' upset you. An opposition fluke, a bad result from your own shot, the condition of the green and the weather can all be perceived as conspiring to beat you. Condition yourself to expect and ignore these irritating factors that you cannot control. Apply zero tolerance for moaning and self-pity. Work out a mental strategy that ensures you cope with these situations.

### Restrain Yourself
Learn to make your own mind up, but also learn when to keep your views to yourself. Listen to experienced views from good players and coaches and test out their theories for yourself. Nobody can guide you in a singles match, so you must be prepared to be your own person. When you are in a team game by all means try to read the head and play, but be careful and tactful how you contribute your views to the rest of your team.

### Avoid Tension
Never become too tense. The perfect competition condition is to have 'a concentrating mind in a relaxed body'. If, however, you feel your arms or legs tensing up before or during a game, then gently shake them loose. Try taking a deep breath before you deliver your bowl. It both helps you to relax and aids concentration.

PART 4

# FITNESS AND WELL-BEING

# CHAPTER II

# EXERCISE AND RECOVERY

## Warm-Up Exercises

While bowls is not usually known for any ingrained dedication to physical preparation, there is no doubt that physical fitness does provide a competitive advantage. Excess body weight and overindulgence are not normally conducive to stimulating the best performances. While I do not wish to concentrate on general fitness routines and healthy lifestyle advice (these are well documented and generally available elsewhere), I would like to focus on some carefully chosen warm-up routines that certainly can benefit your performance. Loosening those joints and muscles prior to play can make a major contribution both to getting off to a good start and reinforcing your stamina for your games, which can last over three hours. Tired limbs and aching joints can have a very detrimental effect on your delivery and concentration. Regular warm-up routines will reduce these unwanted effects.

For our England squad preparation for the Manchester and Melbourne Commonwealth Games it was the pleasure, and privilege, to have the advice and assistance of Rex Hazeldine, a sports scientist at Loughborough University. He is a keen bowler, too, and is currently managing the Nottinghamshire Under-25 squad.

He has very kindly provided me with the following warm-up routines for you to take advantage of. You can use all, or some, of them to help you ensure you are physically well prepared for your games, whether they are practice, recreational or competitive in nature.

Select the warm-up exercise that suits your own personal physical capacity and condition.

## Suggested Warm-Up Routines Prior to Practice and Competition

### Objectives
1 To gradually warm up the body in preparation for play.
2 To stretch the main muscle groups used during your game.
3 To combine the final physical preparation with some mental focus.
4 To be 'warmed up' and ready for play before the trial ends and certainly before the early ends of the match, so you 'hit the ground running'.

### Approach
1 The warm-up routine can be done individually, as a 'team', or together as a squad.
2 Use an appropriate even surface, preferably on grass.
3 Time the warm-up so it is as near to starting the game as possible, but allowing time for all other necessary preparations.

### Flexibility (Stretching)
This maintains or increases the range of movement in the joints. With regular stretching there can be less resistance to movement so a certain degree of energy conservation can be achieved. With the ageing process there is a loss of flexibility (from 20 to 70 years males can lose 40 per cent of flexibility, females a little less). Flexibility is maintained by being active and stretching. A combination of the two is important.

### Routine
The following routine is suggested for bowls but you can add other stretches or exercises, or modify the suggested

routine, to suit your purposes. It is a matter of developing and establishing a warm-up routine that suits you personally and with which you are comfortable.

**Phase 1** To increase body temperature, blood flow and mobilization, walk gently in different directions over a warm-up area and start to loosen neck and shoulders. Then bring your knees up to your chest alternately. Follow this by bringing your knees up to hip level and to the side alternately – this is to loosen the hip joint.

**Phase 2** Easy jogging over short distances (10m). Include some easy astride jumps leading with each shoulder.

**Phase 3** Stretch CALF MUSCLES
*Starting Position* Stand close to and lean on a solid wall (or similar) or partner supporting the body weight on the arms, bend one leg and place the foot in front, with the other leg straight behind (see Fig 39).
*First Movement* Slowly move the hips forward keeping the back flat. Keep the heel of the straight leg firmly on the floor with the toes pointing straight ahead.
*Second Movement* To stretch the lower calf, lower the hips downward as the knees are slightly bending; again, keep the heel down.

**Phase 4** Easy jogging over short distances (10m). Include some 'flicks' by bringing heels up at the back. Also some gentle knee lifts at the front.

**Phase 5** Stretch HAMSTRINGS
*Starting Position* In standing position, place one leg (the leg to be stretched) slightly in front of the other leg. Bend the back leg,

*Fig 39 Gastrocnemius and soleus (calf).*

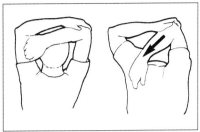

*Fig 42 Arms and shoulders.*

keeping the back straight and using the hands on the back leg to support the spine (see Fig 40). Keep the front leg straight, the head up and prevent the back from curving over.
*Movement* Press forward until you feel a mild tension.

Stretch QUADS
*Starting Position* Stand holding on to something for balance. Flex one knee and raise your heel to the buttocks (see Fig 41).
*Movement* Slightly flex your supporting leg and grasp your raised foot with one hand; slowly pull your heel towards your buttocks without overcompressing the knee.

Stretch SHOULDERS
*Starting Position* Sit or stand legs apart; with arms overhead, hold the elbow of one arm with the hand of the other arm (see Fig 42).
*Movement* Gently pull the elbow behind the head.

**Phase 6** Stretch LOWER BACK
*Starting Position* Sit with legs straight and slightly apart.
*Movement* Fold forward with head down and hands stretched out (see Fig 43).

*Fig 43 Lower back.*

Stretch BUTTOCKS and FRONTS OF HIPS
*Starting Position* Lie on back with legs straight.
*Movement* Draw one knee towards the chest and ease the knee into the chest with your hands (see Fig 44). Change legs. Finally draw both legs together into the chest.

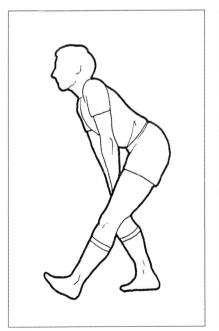

*Fig 40 Hamstrings.*

*Fig 41 Quadriceps.*

*Fig 44 Buttocks and front of hips.*

*Fig 45  Hips and spine.*

**Stretch HIPS and SPINE**
*Starting Position*  In sitting position, cross one leg over the other leg and draw into chest.
*Movement*  Put opposite arm behind the thigh and turn to twist the spine (see Fig 45). Change to other side.

**Stretch LOWER BACK**
*Starting position*  Sit in crossed leg position.
*Movement*  Slowly lean forward, 'walking' the hands out. Back to sitting up. Turn body to one thigh and again lean forward (see Fig 46). Then to the other thigh and do the same movement.

*Fig 46  Lower back.*

**Phase 7**  Finish warm-up routine with LUNGE stretch, alternating with left and right foot forward.
*Starting position*  Place the right foot flat in front; move the right foot forward until the knee is directly over the ankle and the left knee is touching the floor behind, left foot extended.
*Movement*  Lower the hips downward, keeping the hips square to the front; use the hands for balance (see Fig 47). Check that both feet are in line and not turned out.

*Fig 47  Hips and quadriceps.*

# Rest and Recovery During Competition

It is important to plan your rest and recovery during intensive competitions. An all-day tournament, particularly indoors, or longer competitions (e.g. three-day national finals) can be very tiring both physically and mentally. The following advice should help you to maintain your stamina in such circumstances.

- The key factor is to rest your legs. When you are not playing (e.g. between rounds) stay off your feet as much as possible. Avoid walking around. It is also useful to put your feet up horizontally for periods of time to assist the blood flow and allow them to recover effectively.
- Keep in the shade as much as possible if it is hot and sunny.
- After a match it is advisable at some point to undertake some form of light exercise to aid recovery. This should be light and short in duration: jogging on the spot, for example, should be enough to get the circulation going, followed by a little stretching to help move waste products, which will have accumulated during the previous match, away from the muscles.

# Getting a Good Night's Sleep

Unfortunately, many people find it difficult to get a good night's sleep before a big game. The following advice, which was given to the England Commonwealth Games bowls squad, may help.

Getting to sleep is a bit like learning to relax – the harder you try the more impossible it becomes! So stop trying. If you are lying awake in bed your body is still resting and recovering from exercise.

Now it's time to check out why you are not asleep – once you know why, you can do something about it. Listed below are some common reasons for not sleeping and some strategies you can try.

1. You don't feel tired (maybe due to going to bed earlier/later than usual).
   - Don't worry, your body will gain the benefit of restful sleep by lowering its activation level. You can read a book, listen to music, practise some imagery or anything else that does not get you up and about.

2. You feel physically tired but mentally alert.
   - As above, don't worry, your body needs rest but you can gain all the physical benefits while quietly awake.

3. You are very tired but can't seem to switch off the thoughts going through my mind. There are a number of things you can try:
   - Listen to one of the deep muscular relaxation tapes. This is useful if you feel physically tense, but will often give your mind a more appropriate focus for sleeping.
   - Keep a notepad and pencil handy and write down the thoughts running through your mind. Having committed your thoughts to paper you will often be able to 'let them go'.
   - If you are feeling anxious about the coming match repeat some positive self-affirmations by recalling some of your best bowling shots/moments.
   - Remind yourself that you can only do your best.

# EPILOGUE

*A colourful England supporter being welcomed by the England Team Manager, John Bell, to the British Isles team championships at the impressive Wigton Bowls Club. Enjoy your bowls and savour the best moments.*
(Courtesy of Bowls International)

I have done my best to provide you with sound guidance and advice on the techniques and skills that you need to get the best out of your bowling activity. I have also highlighted some of the players who have demonstrated these skills with particular effect, and who have achieved the highest honours in the game.

Our great game, though, is all-embracing. It can be played competently and absorbingly at a number of levels where the varying needs and aspirations of individuals can all be satisfied. Whatever level that is, you will only derive the ultimate pleasure out of bowls if you master the very basic rudiments involved in it. There is no doubt they are well worth pursuing, particularly in the

knowledge that there is a lot of coaching and technical support available. Whether it be friendly club play, competitions and tournaments, or international matchplay, there will always be the opportunity to experience and savour many memorable and enjoyable moments. These will be shared with a vast cross-section of largely agreeable individuals, who might be extremely competitive during their games, but who also fully subscribe to the game's unwritten code of strong camaraderie off the green, and good sportsmanship on it.

I wish you well with the development, improvement and, above all, the enjoyment of your game, to which I hope this book will make a meaningful contribution.

For the Good Times

*Camaraderie at the Tri-Nations Tournament in Perth in October 2005: Jim Baker, John Bell and Andy Thomson enjoying the moment.*
(© John Bell)

# THE GAME OF BOWLS – OTHER POPULAR DERIVATIONS

## Federation Bowls

This is a flat green game similar to the game described in this book. It is currently played in thirteen English counties: Cleveland, Derbyshire, Durham, Humberside, Huntingdonshire, Lincolnshire, Norfolk, Northamptonshire, North Cambridgeshire, North Essex, Northumberland, Nottinghamshire and Suffolk. Its main variations from the normal flat green game are:

• there are no touchers;
• bowls have to be within 2m of the jack to count;
• players can change position within their teams (pairs, triples);
• there is no fours discipline.

English Bowling Federation (EBF)
John Heppel
Secretary
14 Field Close
Worksop, Nottinghamshire
S81 0PF
Tel/Fax: 01909 474346
email: j.heppel@btinternet.com
web: www.fedbowls.co.uk

## Crown Green Bowls

This popular variation is not a flat green game. It is played on a green that rises in height to a crown approximately 225–300mm above the level of its edges. Both the bowls and jack are biased and play is not restricted to 'rinks'. The jack can be bowled almost anywhere on the green. All players use two bowls and only singles and pairs games are played. The game is largely played in the North of England (Yorkshire, Cheshire, Cumbria and Lancashire, including Merseyside and Greater Manchester), the Midlands (Derbyshire, North Midlands, the Potteries, Shropshire, Staffordshire, Warwick and Worcester), North Wales and the Isle of Man.

British Crown Green Bowling Association (BCGBA)
John Crowther
Chief Executive
94 Fishers Lane, Pensby
Wirral, Merseyside
CH61 8SB
Tel: 01516 485740
Fax: 01516 480733
web: www.bowls.org

## Short Mat Bowls

This is a major variation to our indoor flat green game. It is played on a mat measuring only 12.2–13.75m long and 1.83m wide using normal sized bowls. A block of wood is placed halfway along the mat and in the centre of it. This prevents 'heavy' shots being played up the middle of the mat. There is a simulated ditch and a minimum distance that the bowls must travel in order for them to be deemed 'live'. It is a popular community activity in church halls, village halls and bowls clubhouses where space is restricted. The short mat game has proved very successful in introducing new players to the game of bowls, and is played throughout the UK.

English Short Mat Bowling Association (ESMBA)
Herbie Bowden
General Secretary
Wytheford Hall Farm
Shawbury, Shropshire
SY4 4JJ
Tel: 01952 770218
email: esmbaadmin@hotmail.com
web: www.esmba.org.uk

## Carpet Bowls

This is very similar in concept to the short mat game, except that the mat is shorter (around 9.2m) and there is no 'ditch'. The bowls are also a lot smaller than the normal ones used in all the other games.

# GLOSSARY

**Back bowl** Generally regarded as a bowl that finishes behind the head.

**Backhand** The left-hand side of the rink (for a right-handed bowler taking stance on the mat) where a bowl will bend from left to right towards the centre line. Opposite way round for left-handers.

**Bank** The raised area containing and surrounding the ditch and green.

**Bare length** Term used to describe a bowl that is just short of the jack length.

**Be up** (or **don't be short**) Emphasizing the need to reach the head.

**Bias** That which determines how much a bowl will bend on its path to its target. (The shape of the bowl determines how strong the bias will be. There are now many variations of bias to suit the varying playing conditions encountered.)

**Blocker** A bowl deliberately played short of the head in order to protect a favourable position there, and prevent an opponent from getting access to that position by *blocking* his shot.

**Bowl(s)** Bowls are acquired in sets of four – all four bowls are identical and of the same manufacture. They must be the same size, weight, colour and bias, and have the same serial number and engraving. In all games each player must play with the appropriate number of bowls from the *same set*.

**Draw** The art of delivering a bowl with, in particular, the *right weight*, along with a good line, so that it comes to rest in the immediate area for which it is intended.

**Draw the shot** Instruction to use the *correct weight* and line in order to get your bowl closest to the jack.

**Drive (fire)** A shot played with great force.

**End** Whatever discipline is being played – singles, pairs, triples or fours – the game consists of individual 'ends'. Each time all the players have played all their bowls in one direction it constitutes an 'end' played. An 'end' begins with placing the mat and

delivering the jack. It is completed after the last bowl has been played. If the jack is knocked outside the confines of the rink then the end is normally replayed in the same direction (unless agreed otherwise by the skips). Also see **Respotted jack**.

**Extra end** If the scores are level after the designated number of ends have been played, an extra end is played to determine a winner. Irrespective of who won the last end of the game, both sides toss for jack before the commencement of the extra end.

**Fast green** One where the speed of the green is adjudged to be 15/16 seconds and above. (The speed relates to the time taken for a bowl to cover 27m). Many indoor clubs have fast greens.

**Fluke** A lucky shot.

**Follow through** The desired 'follow through' of the delivery arm along the line of the delivered bowl.

**Foot fault** Where the rear foot* (or part thereof **) is not on or above the mat at the moment the bowl is delivered from the hand (* BIBC ruling; ** WB Ltd ruling).

**Forehand** The right-hand side of the rink (for a right-handed bowler taking stance on the mat) where a bowl will bend from right to left towards the centre line.

**Green** The total playing surface, which is divided up into rinks for match play.

**Take the green** Instruction to remind bowlers to take a line that allows their bowls to fully bend and not to take a line that is too narrow.

**Slow** or **heavy green** Where the conditions (it could be long or thick grass, wet weather or thick underlay) affect the free running of the bowls and slow them down. During play it normally involves taking a narrower line and delivering with more weight.

**Head** Normally the wide area around the jack where the majority of bowls accumulate at any given end.

**Heavy bowl** A bowl delivered with weight. It can be intentional or not.

**Jack (kitty, white)** The white (or it can be yellow) ball is the centre of attention in the game of bowls. The vast majority of play is directed towards it and the scoring system is totally related to how close bowls can get to it. Each end commences with the delivery of the jack.

**Jack high (level) bowl** A bowl that has come to rest at a point that is the same distance from the mat as the jack.

**Land** (also **green**) Refers to the delivery line 'Give it plenty land', meaning to make sure the delivery line is wide enough to allow the bowl to bend properly.

**Last bowl** As it suggests, the last bowl to be played in any end. The player holding the last bowl may, however, opt not to play it if he considers the head/position too dangerous.

**Lead** The player who lays the mat, delivers the jack and plays the first bowl for his team at the commencement of an end.

**Live bowl** Any bowl that is active during an end and which can have an influence in the outcome of that end – no matter in how bizarre a fashion! A live bowl is one that is within the confines of the rink (if it is in the ditch, it must have touched the jack to be still alive).

**Long jack** Where the jack is delivered to a point on or close to the 2m mark at the opposite end of the rink.

**Mark (chalk) it** To mark a bowl with chalk (or white spray) to indicate it has touched the jack.

**Marker** A person who officiates in a game of singles to ensure it is played in accordance with the Laws of the Sport.

**Mat** Bowlers must deliver their bowls from a mat. It can be positioned in a variety of places along the centre line of the rink as long as it is a minimum of 2m from the ditch edge and there is a minimum of 23m between it and the jack.

**Measure** A device used to measure the distances between bowls and the jack in order to determine which are nearest.

**Narrow** Where a player has missed the correct line by not giving his bowl enough 'green'/'land'. This results in him playing a 'narrow' bowl, which will finish inside his intended target.

**Open it up (play through)** An instruction often given by skips to their thirds when an unfavourable head has developed. The drawing hands may be blocked and a weight shot is required to open the head up to give the skip a better chance to see the jack and retrieve the situation.

**Pace (weight)** The amount of force with which a bowl is delivered. This will vary with the particular shot that is required.

**Pace of the green** How fast/slow the green is running.

**Pairs game** Two players, normally using four bowls, playing against another pair.

**Plant** A shot that hits one bowl (primary bowl) into another (secondary bowl) with the specific purpose of using the secondary bowl to achieve your objective.

**Promote a bowl** Common practice in which a weighted bowl is played on to one, or more, short bowls to 'promote' them into the head and/or onto the jack.

**Push and rest (chop and lie)** Another carefully weighted shot to 'push' an opposition bowl out of the head and stop in its place.

**Respotted jack** In certain games (e.g. in domestic tournaments, TV tournaments) when the jack is knocked out of the rink it is 'respotted' on a designated mark – normally 1m in from the boundary line of the rink and 2m from the edge of the ditch. This 'respotting' is undertaken instead of replaying the end. It saves time and maintains continuity of play.

**Rest this bowl** An instruction to play just over the draw to push gently on to a bowl and rest inside it.

**Rink** The rectangular division of the green used for individual games.

**Rink (fours)** A team of four players, playing with two bowls each – lead, second, third and skip.

**Rub/Wick** Where a bowl comes into contact with the edge of another bowl and changes its line into/past the head.

**Scorer** Person who keeps the scoreboard(s) at the end of the rinks, or master scoreboards.

**Second (Number 2)** The player who plays second in a rink (fours side) or triple.

**Sets play** A match format largely involving singles play. Initiated for TV tournaments and now extended to other selected competitions. The outcome of the game is determined by playing 2 (or 3) sets of a designated number of ends. If, in the case of a 2-set contest, the score is 1 set all after the end of the second set, then a tie breaker end or tie breaker ends (3) is/are played to determine a winner.

**Short bowl** A bowl that has not reached the head/jack.

**Short jack** A jack that is delivered to a point that is at, or just over, the minimum distance permitted (23m).

**Shot bowl** The bowl that is nearest to the jack.

**Shoulder of the green** The point on the running line of a bowl where it begins to curve inwards towards its target.

**Singles** A head to head game between one player and another – normally using four bowls. The format can either be 21 shots up or a sets game.

**Skip** The motivator, tactician and skilled player who commands his fellow players in pairs, triples and fours games. He is last to bowl and dictates the strategies for the games played.

**Stance** The position adopted on the mat prior to delivery.

**Strings** Used to define the boundaries of the rink.

**Take out** A heavily weighted shot played to remove an opponent's bowl from the head or green.

**Third** This person plays third in a fours side (rink). He is deputy skip.

**Tie breaker** An end, or ends, played in a sets match when the set scores are level. In the case of three tie break ends being played, the winner of each end scores one point only, irrespective of the number of shots he holds.

**Tied end** This occurs when the closest bowls of each side are exactly the same distance from the jack at the completion of the end, e.g. both bowls touching the jack. In this event neither side scores a shot but the end is deemed to have been played and entered onto the scorecard as such.

**Toucher** A bowl that has touched the jack during its course. It must touch the jack before the next bowl is delivered or, if it is the last bowl, before a period of 30 seconds has elapsed. Such bowls will be marked with chalk/white spray.

**Toucher (in the ditch)** A toucher that ends up in the ditch is still a 'live' bowl as long as it is within the confines of the rink.

**Trail (the Jack)** Playing a bowl that 'picks' up the jack and moves it to another position in the rink. A 'trail' shot normally implies that the jack stays largely with the bowl.

**Triples** A team of three players who normally play with three bowls.

**Umpire** The main official at any game, responsible for enforcing the Laws of the Sport.

**Using the mat** Moving the mat to various positions up and down the centre line of the rink in order to lengthen/shorten the length of the jack.

**Wide bowl** A bowl played with too much green/land, which finishes wide of its target.

**Wrecked** A bowl that makes contact with another bowl and is stopped from fulfilling its objective.

# USEFUL CONTACTS

The following information was correct at the time of going to press, but personnel and other details may change over time.

## Key Administrative Bodies

World Bowls Ltd
Gary Smith
Chief Executive
Sportscotland
Caledonia House
1 Redheughs Rigg
South Gyle
Edinburgh, EH12 9DQ
Tel: 0131 3179764
Fax: 0131 3179765
email: worldbowls@btconnect.com
web: www.worldbowlsltd.com

British Isles Bowls Council
Michael Swatland
Hon. Secretary
23 Leysland Avenue
Countesthorpe, Leicester
LE8 5XX
Tel: 0116 2773234
email: michaelswatland@btinternet.com
web: www.britishislesbowls.com

Bowls England
Tony Allcock
Chief Executive
Lyndhurst Road
Worthing, West Sussex
BN11 2AZ
Tel: 01903 820222
Fax: 01903 820444
email: tony@bowlsengland.com
web: www.bowlsengland.com

Bowls England is the new unified body representing the former English Bowling Association (EBA) and English Women's Bowling Association (EWBA).

English Indoor Bowling Association (EIBA)
Steve Rodwell
Secretary
EIBA Headquarters
David Cornwell House
Bowling Green, Leicester Road
Melton Mowbray, Leicestershire
LE13 0FA
Tel: 01664 481900
Fax: 01664 482888
email: Stever@eiba.co.uk
web: www.eiba.co.uk

English Women's Indoor Bowling Association (EWIBA)
Mrs Tricia Thomas
National Secretary
3 Moulton Business Park
Scirocco Close, Northampton
NN3 6AP
Tel: 01604 494163
Fax: 01604 494434
email: ewiba@btconnect.com
web: www.ewiba.com

European Bowls Union (EBU)
R. (Bob) Jack FCA
Secretary/Treasurer
Woodville, 14 Treesdale Close
Birkdale, Southport, Merseyside
PR8 2EL
Tel/Fax: 01704 553574
email: bobjackeba@hotmail.com
web: www.europeanbowlsunion.com

World Indoor Bowls Council (WIBC)
Liz Read
Secretary
122 Oxford Road
Kidlington, Oxon
OX5 1DZ
Tel: 01865 372910
email: lizread5@hotmail.com
web: www.wibc.org.uk

British Isles Indoor Bowls Council (BIIBC)
Brian Davies
Hon. Secretary/Treasurer
16 Hendre Avenue
Ogmore Vale, Bridgend
CF32 7HD
Tel: 01656 841361
Fax: 01656 849160
email: briandaviesbowls@btinternet.com
web: www.biibc.org.uk

Association of Irish Indoor Bowls (AIIB)
Cecil Davidson
Hon. Secretary
12 Moss Road, Newtownabbey
BT36 5JY
Tel/Fax: 02890 286664 or 02890 835780

Irish Women's Indoor Bowling Association (IWIBA)
Mrs Doreen Miskelly
Hon. Secretary
101 Skyline Drive
Lamberg, Lisbern, County Antrim
BT27 4HW
Tel: 02892 663516
Fax: 02892 587389

Irish Bowling Association (IBA)
Tom Mcgarel
Secretary
2 Oronsay Crescent, Larne
BT40 2HD
Tel/Fax: 02828 270008
email: irishbowling@btinternet.com
web: www.irishlawnbowls.ie

Scottish Indoor Bowling Association (SIBA)
Gordon Woods
Hon. Secretary
1 Nursery Lane
Mauchline, Ayrshire
KA5 6EH
Tel/Fax: 01290 551067
web: www.bowls-siba.co.uk

Scottish Women's Indoor Bowling Association
(SWIBA)
Mrs Anne Easton
Hon. Secretary
Troscons, Watson Street
Letham, Forfar
DD8 2QB
Tel: 01307 818238
web: members.lycos.co.uk/stewart41/swiba.htm

Scottish Bowling Association (SBA)
Ian Pickavance
Secretary
National Centre for Bowling
Northfield
Hunters Avenue, Ayr
KA8 9AL
Tel/Fax: 01292 294623
email: scottishbowling@aol.com
web: www.scottish-bowling.co.uk

Scottish Women's Bowling Association (SWBA)
Mrs Anna Marshall
Secretary
Unit 76, S.T.E.P.
John Player Building
Stirling
SK7 7RP
Tel: 01786 449012
Fax: 01324 873428
email: SWBA76@aol.com

Welsh Indoor Bowls Association (WIBA)
David Phillips
Hon. Secretary
50 Penyrheol Road
Gorseinon, Swansea
SA4 4GA
Tel: 01792 538061
Fax: 01792 548221
web: www.welshindoorbowls.com

Welsh Ladies Indoor Bowling Association
(WLIBA)
Mrs Hilary King
Secretary
Hillcrest Villa
Tynewydd, Treorchy
CF42 5LU
Tel: 01443 771618
email: Secretary@wliba.com
web: www.wliba.com

Welsh Bowling Association (WBA)
Jim Ireland
Secretary
6 Nordale Court
Fidlas Road, Cardiff
CF14 5NJ
Tel: 02920 634995
email: j.ireland@ntlworld.com
web: www.welshbowlingassociation.co.uk

Welsh Women's Bowling Association (WWBA)
Miss Linda Parker MBE
Secretary
Ffrydd Cottage
2 Ffrydd Road
Knighton, Powys
LD7 1DB
Tel/Fax: 01547 528331

English Bowls Players' Association (EBPA)
Carol Ashby
Secretary/Treasurer
6 Pensford Drive
Eastbourne, East Sussex
BN23 7NY
Tel: 07976 956799
Fax: 01323 461406
email: carolashby@btinternet.com
web: www.ebpa.co.uk

Professional Bowls Association (PBA)
Wynne Richards
Secretary/Treasurer
Tricklewood View
Cosheston
Pembroke Dock, Dyfed
SA72 4UD
Tel: 01646 681760
email: wynne@bowlspba.com
web: www.bowlspba.com /
www.worldbowlstour.com

Bowls Guernsey Association
Garry Collins
Chief Executive
88 Victoria Road
St Peter Port, Guernsey
GY1 1JB
Tel: 01481 717325
Fax: 01481 717124
email: garry.collins@gov.gg
web: www.bowlsguernsey.org

Isle of Man Flat Green Bowling Club
Mrs Pauline Kelly
Secretary
14 Hilltop Rise
Farmhill
Douglas, Isle of Man
IM2 2LE
Tel: 01624 676931
email: mikeandpaulinekelly@manx.net

Bowls Jersey
Mrs Gail Boswell
Secretary
Les Brises
Route des Genets
St Brelade, Jersey
JE3 8LE
Tel/Fax: 01534 747822
email: gailboswell50@hotmail.com
web: bowlsjersey.org.je

# World Bowls

Bowls Australia Inc
Neil Dalrymple
Chief Executive Officer
PO Box 6087
Hawthorne West
Victoria 3122, Australia
Tel: 61 3 9819 2722
email: mrendell@bowls-australia.com.au
web: www.bowls-aus.com.au

Bowls New Zealand Inc
P.K. Clark OBE
Chief Executive
PO Box 62502
Central Park
Auckland 1130, New Zealand
Tel: 64 9 579 5853
email: kerry@bowlsnz.co.nz
web: www.bowlsnz.co.nz

# Other Useful Contacts

The English Bowls Coaching Scheme
web: www.englishbowlscoaching.com

Regional Coach – Southern Region
Julia Creswell
82 Main Road
Littleton
Winchester
SO22 6QS
Tel: 01962 881697

Regional Coach – Midlands Region
Peter Harris
70 Banbury Road
Brackley, Northants
NN13 6AJ
Tel: 01280 706318

Regional Coach – Southwest Region
Gwyn John
'Gower'
34 Ocean View Road
Bude, Cornwall
EX23 8NN
Tel: 01288 352391

Regional Coach – Northern Region
Brian Warren
Gilston House
West Street
Wigton, Cumbria
CA7 9NX
Tel: 01697 349265

Regional Coach – East Anglia Region
Arthur Meeson
22 Pleasant Rise
Hatfield, Herts
AL9 5DU
Tel: 01707 268081

Regional Coach – Central Region
Vic Waite
19 Recreation Road
Wargrove
Reading, Berks
RG10 8BG
Tel: 01189 402334

## *Licensed Bowls Manufacturers and Testers*

Thomas Taylor (Bowls) Ltd
217 Bernard Street
Glasgow
G40 3NB
Tel: 0141 554 5255
email: info@taylor-bowls.co.uk

Bowls Direct Ltd
66 Francis Road
Omokoroa RD2
Tauranga
New Zealand
Tel: 07 548 0330
email: bowls@bowlsdirect.co.nz

George Mackay
65 Blackfriars Street
Edinburgh
EH1 1NB
Tel: 0131 556 1779

Bowls International (Pty) Ltd
245 Nicklin Way
Warana
Queensland 4575
Australia
Tel: 07 5493 2293
email: bowlsinternational@primus.co.au

Henselite (Australia) Pty Ltd
320 Darebin Road
PO Box 197
Fairfield, Victoria 3078
Australia
Tel: 03 9488 0488
email: enquiries@henselite.co.au

Pershore Bowls Centre
Units 5B & C
Pershore Trading Estate
Pershore, Worcs
WR10 2DD
Tel: 01386 552 411
email: pershorebc@btconnect.com

Sydney Bowls Centre
11a Elizabeth Street
Campsie
NSW 2194
Australia
Tel: 02 9789 4400

email: sydneybowls@aol.com
Fred Fern's Bowls Centre Pty Ltd
Unit 2, 16 Nile Street
Woolloongabba
Queensland 4102
Australia
Tel: 07 3391 5222
email: ferng@fredfern.com.au

Drakes Pride
72 Powells Avenue
Bendigo
Victoria 3550
Australia
Tel: 03 5443 7133
email: drakespride@netcon.net.au

Greenmaster Bowls (Australia) Pty Ltd
Unit 5, 1 Boden Road
Seven Hills
NSW 2147
Australia
Tel: 02 9674 7777
email: greenmaster@swiftdsl.com.au

Drakes Pride
128 Richmond Row
Liverpool
L3 3BL
Tel: 0151 298 1355
email: drakespride@eaclare.freenetname.co.uk

**English Bowls Umpires Association**

Chairman:
Peter Price
Heatherdean Green Lane
Farnham Common
Slough
SL2 3SP

Deputy Chairman:
Jim Barlow
44D Dean Road
Bittern Village
Southampton
SO18 6AP
Tel: 02380 448821

# INDEX